# GOD IS YOUR DEFENDER

# GOD IS YOUR DEFENDER

**LEARNING
TO STAND**
AFTER
LIFE HAS
KNOCKED
YOU DOWN

# ROSIE RIVERA

W PUBLISHING GROUP

AN IMPRINT OF THOMAS NELSON

*God Is Your Defender*

© 2021 Samalia, Inc.

Published in Nashville, Tennessee, by W Publishing, an imprint of Thomas Nelson.

Thomas Nelson titles may be purchased in bulk for educational, business, fundraising, or sales promotional use. For information, please email SpecialMarkets@ThomasNelson.com.

Unless otherwise noted, Scripture quotations are taken from the Holy Bible, New International Version®, NIV®. Copyright © 1973, 1978, 1984, 2011 by Biblica, Inc.® Used by permission of Zondervan. All rights reserved worldwide. www.Zondervan.com. The "NIV" and "New International Version" are trademarks registered in the United States Patent and Trademark Office by Biblica, Inc.®

Scripture quotations marked AMP are taken from the Amplified® Bible (AMP). Copyright © 2015 by The Lockman Foundation. Used by permission. www.Lockman.org

Scripture quotations marked ESV are taken from the ESV® Bible (The Holy Bible, English Standard Version®). Copyright © 2001 by Crossway, a publishing ministry of Good News Publishers. Used by permission. All rights reserved.

Scripture quotations marked KJV are taken from the King James Version. Public domain.

Scripture quotations marked THE MESSAGE are taken from THE MESSAGE. Copyright © 1993, 2002, 2018 by Eugene H. Peterson. Used by permission of NavPress. All rights reserved. Represented by Tyndale House Publishers, a Division of Tyndale House Ministries.

Scripture quotations marked NASB are taken from the New American Standard Bible® (NASB). Copyright © 1960, 1962, 1963, 1968, 1971, 1972, 1973, 1975, 1977, 1995 by The Lockman Foundation. Used by permission. www.Lockman.org

Scripture quotations marked NKJV are taken from the New King James Version®. Copyright © 1982 by Thomas Nelson. Used by permission. All rights reserved.

Scripture quotations marked NLT are taken from the Holy Bible, New Living Translation. © 1996, 2004, 2015 by Tyndale House Foundation. Used by permission of Tyndale House Publishers, Inc., Carol Stream, Illinois 60188. All rights reserved.

Scripture quotations marked NOG are taken from The Names of God Bible (without notes). Copyright © 2011 by Baker Publishing Group.

Scripture quotations marked RSV are taken from the Revised Standard Version of the Bible. Copyright © 1946, 1952, and 1971 National Council of the Churches of Christ in the United States of America. Used by permission. All rights reserved.

Scripture quotations marked TLB are taken from The Living Bible. Copyright © 1971. Used by permission of Tyndale House Publishers, a Division of Tyndale House Ministries, Carol Stream, Illinois 60188. All rights reserved.

Scripture quotations marked TPT are from The Passion Translation®. Copyright © 2017, 2018 by Passion & Fire Ministries, Inc. Used by permission. All rights reserved. ThePassionTranslation.com.

ISBN 978-0-7852-3777-8 (audiobook)
ISBN 978-0-7852-3775-4 (eBook)
ISBN 978-0-7852-3772-3 (HC)
ISBN 978-0-7852-9028-5 (SE)

**Library of Congress Cataloging-in-Publication Data**
Library of Congress Control Number: 2020952510

*Printed in the United States of America*

21 22 23 24 25  LSC  10 9 8 7 6 5 4 3 2 1

*For my brother Juanelo and my husband,
Abel, for all the times you wanted to defend
me with your fists but instead got on your
knees and prayed for God to defend me.*

# CONTENTS

# FOREWORD

THE BOOK YOU HOLD IN YOUR HANDS—OR ARE READ-ing on the screen of your choice, as the case may be—is a challenge.

It's a challenge to embrace God's promise to Moses in Exodus 14:14: "The Lord will fight for you; you need only to be still." It's a challenge to embrace God's promise to you.

And Rosie Rivera is no stranger to a challenge.

Rosie is a survivor. She openly shares her experience of abuse as a child and the tragic loss of her sister, internationally acclaimed singer Jenni Rivera, in a plane crash in 2012. Despite the hurt she has faced, she refuses to be beaten down or silenced by the Enemy.

Why?

Because she knows God is her Defender.

When Rosie asked me to write the foreword for this book, I was humbled. Rosie is one of the most influential and inspirational Latinas in the world. She cohosts *The Power of Us*, a marriage podcast with her husband, Abel; she mothers three precious children; and she has now authored five books. She is a wife, mother, author, and influencer. She uses what the Enemy intended for evil as an opportunity to glorify God and create good. She founded Sister Samalia, an organization that supports girls and women trapped in the cycle of abuse, so they can experience God's healing as she has.

Rosie is a woman of immense strength and faith because she takes God at his word. That is her daily challenge to herself, and that is her challenge to you and me.

With conviction and compassion, humor and honesty, Rosie

shares with us how she learned to allow God to fight for her, trusting that he will win, every time. She invites us along with her on her journey toward wholeness, teaching us where the true battle lies, ways in which we try to act as our own defenders, and how we can finally place our struggles and sorrows in God's hands and leave them there.

If you are tired of fighting, then *God Is Your Defender* is for you.

—Rev. Samuel Rodriguez

Lead Pastor, New Season Church

President, NHCLC

Author of *From Survive to Thrive: Live a Holy, Healed, Healthy, Happy, Humble, Hungry, and Honoring Life*

Executive Producer, *Breakthrough* (2019)

# INTRODUCTION

IT WAS A PERFECT SOUTHERN CALIFORNIA EVENING. Clear skies. A few hours left of soft sunshine before sunset over the Pacific. No humidity, an outdoor temp set at just right—not too hot, not too cold. A Goldilocks kind of end to the day.

I'm not trying to brag, mind you. Look, I can't help it that California delivers up this kind of delightful evening.

I was heading to the Little League field, ready to watch my godson play baseball at his favorite position of pitcher. The heavenly scent of corn dogs, yeasty giant pretzels, and buttery popcorn from the snack stand made a perfect evening even better. It's been my experience that junk food tastes better at a ballpark, am I right? And I like to think the calories don't count.

It had been a long, stressful day at work. I'd been cooped up inside, managing some difficult phone calls and grinding through what felt like a hundred critical decisions. I love my work, but there are days it's all-consuming. I needed some fresh air and some time away from my phone, my computer, my desk, and the urgency of business. I was looking forward to putting all that aside and immersing myself in what felt like such a happy, innocent pastime: cheering on my godson, chatting with the other spectators, and enjoying the simple joys of little kids dressed in their ball jerseys, celebrating the little wins.

The first time my godson took t mvhe mound to pitch, I heard her: a mom with a kid on the opposing team. She was wearing all their swag: a parent jersey bedecked and bedazzled in rhinestones, a bright ball cap secured over her wild hair. And she was loud. She started bawling at the child who was up to bat, hollering instructions and opinions about how he should swing at the ball. Then she yelled unkind things about my godson's team. A lot of the other parents around me started shifting uncomfortably on the grooved metal benches of the bleacher stands, looking down the row at her. It's such an awkward thing when people raise their voices and change an environment from what has felt good natured into something with a hint of hostility to it. We were a sea of uneasy spectators breathing the fumes of an unfiltered mouth. I started thinking of her as Mama Yeller, and she was living up to her name.

The kid up to bat got a base hit and made his way to first base. We supporters of my godson's team clapped politely. The opposing team's supporters understandably made a more enthusiastic noise of support. And then Mama Yeller started again, her loud commentary echoing down the row.

"That's right!" she hollered. "You show 'em! They're weak!"

Um, ouch. Her content was starting to outpace her volume, which was saying something.

The first inning wrapped up, and I resolved to ignore the loud distraction down the row, determined to not allow this woman to undermine the happiness of a giant pretzel smeared in mustard and one of my favorite kiddos playing his heart out. I wouldn't let some person with no filter and no apparent understanding of polite volume control ruin my evening. After all, I'd earned it, considering the day I'd had at work. *Just relax, Rosie,* I told myself. *It's a good night. Look at that gathering sunset. Breathe in the buttered popcorn perfume from the snack stand and breathe out the growing irritation with Mama Yeller. Breathe in. Breathe out.*

It almost worked. Almost.

In the fifth inning, with my godson back on the pitcher's

mound, Mama Yeller's own son took his stance as the batter. My patience had worn thin—and the wheels came off.

She started yelling insults about my godson.

"He's got nothing you can't hit! He's no pitcher! You got this, son! Kill it! He's a loser!" Mama Yeller had just turned the corner into making this personal, and this girl, your Rosie, switched in an instant to livid.

Now, I aim to be a patient, empathetic person. I want to respond to people the way I believe Jesus would. I want to be the more mature person in any interaction. I want to take the high road. I've walked with God a long time. He's seen me through some pretty horrific stuff, certainly situations more traumatic and dramatic than some stranger yelling at my godson. But it was too much, Mama Yeller and her very targeted attack on a child I love as my own. I started to get to my feet, ready to give her a piece of my mind about her tacky jersey and her big mouth and crazy hair and her origins in general. I was ready to right this wrong and felt a sense of righteous indignation take hold. It was time to defend, time to set things right, time for vengeance.

And then came that whisper, that truth I know and struggle to remember and believe sometimes: *God is your Defender.*

*I know*, I thought. *But this is just craziness. This woman is ruining the night! Someone should do something, and I can be the one!*

*God is your Defender.*

I kept my backside planted on the bench of the bleacher, while my feet itched to jump into the fray. *It's not fair!* I raged internally. *Why do people act like this?*

*God is your Defender.*

Ultimately, I didn't get up, didn't march down the bleachers, didn't put her in her place, shut her up, shut her down. I'd like to tell you it's because I've got such a mature grip on this spiritual walk of mine. But, to be honest, I was mainly concerned that if I said anything to her, I'd end up fighting her. Not just verbally. No, ma'am. I was ready to come off that bench and physically take her down. Images of plowing her into the ground danced in my mind, the dust of the ball field rising as a cloud like the incense of vindication, which would make sense poetically, since I was incensed.

How like Jesus of me.

## THREE QUESTIONS

### WHY DO BAD THINGS HAPPEN?

I've faced some really big hurts in my life. Seriously big. And I've faced some smaller ones, too, like that Little League spectator who was doing her best to ruin a perfectly lovely Southern California round of baseball. In all of it comes this question: Why do bad things happen?

Big or small, bad things invade our sense of peace. They rob us of our sure footing, leaving us dizzy and reeling in their wake.

When those hurts come, they can activate what psychologists say is one of our more basic instincts: the desire for revenge.

We call it by many names. Vindication. Justice. Revenge. Retribution. Retaliation. Vengeance.

If it's any comfort, some of the Hall of Famers of the Bible struggled with all of these desires, this drive to call out their enemies and fix things.

There's a fancy ten-dollar theology phrase for the kind of writing that expresses this desire for revenge. It's called an *imprecatory psalm*, and it means those places in Scripture where someone is calling down the destruction of their enemies, wishing all kinds of calamity and chaos on those who have hurt them. Theologians say that imprecatory psalms were prayers, as opposed to how we commonly think of the majority of the psalms as songs. Here's a list of the major imprecatory psalms, should you care to check them out: Psalm 5, 10, 17, 35, 58, 59, 69, 70, 79, 83, 109, 129, 137, and 140. Of these fourteen imprecatory psalms, David wrote nine of them, which means that more than 70 percent of these "retribution" psalms were written by the person Scripture calls "a man after [God's] own heart" (1 Sam. 13:14). David's life—from the overlooked younger brother in a big family, to the kid sent out to watch over the family flocks, to the famed shepherd boy who took down the giant Goliath, to the young man who served as musician to King Saul, to the man who endured all the conflict and hurt and commotion of his path to the throne of Israel—warranted plenty of opportunities to look for justice and vengeance. And David didn't mince words in his written cries to God. One of my favorite (and one of the most dramatic) imprecatory psalms is Psalm 35:

> May those who seek my life
>     be disgraced and put to shame;
> may those who plot my ruin
>     be turned back in dismay.
> May they be like chaff before the wind,
>     with the angel of the LORD driving them away;
> may their path be dark and slippery,
>     with the angel of the LORD pursuing them.
>
> Since they hid their net for me without cause
>     and without cause dug a pit for me,
> may ruin overtake them by surprise—

> may the net they hid entangle them,
>
> may they fall into the pit, to their ruin.
>
> Then my soul will rejoice in the LORD
>
> and delight in his salvation. (vv. 4–9)

I mean, wow. Those are some fightin' words. And it is in David's imprecatory psalms that I find I most often resonate with him, with the things he battled in his life, with his powerful emotions as he processed the challenges and enemies and deceit and plots that came against him.

I often see David ask in his psalms why his enemies are so cruel. He asked why God hadn't responded yet. He asked when things would be set right, when a season of peace would prevail. He asked many of the same things I ask when I'm battered and bruised by the actions of others, when I'm hurting and wounded. It's not lost on me that David arrived at no conclusion other than that God is good, and good will win. And he often referred to God as Defender. Protector. Shield.

Jehovah El Elyon.

We don't have the answer to why bad things happen. It's beyond you, and it's beyond me. Sometimes a preacher might try to simplify this and tell you that if you'd just had enough faith, you wouldn't have been hurt. He might tell you there was something in your behavior or attitude that brought this bad thing about. Don't listen to that mess. Bad things happen that are not your fault. Period. But here's something I've finally learned: I don't have to have the answer for why bad things happen. What I do need to have, rock solid in my core, is this foundational truth: good always wins. I've settled that in my heart. I've decided. So then two questions follow, the first of which is critical.

## AM I GOING TO LET EVIL WIN IN ME?

I can practically hear your next questions. They are the same ones I wrestle with when it comes to taking a stand for what is right and allowing God to be my Defender. When should I step in? How should I do it? When am I being a coward, and when am I being courageous? What does it look like when I allow God to be my Defender? We're going to explore all of that in the following chapters and try to make some sense of the internal struggle in situations that so often don't make sense in our lives. We're going to explore the areas where seeking revenge, seeking to right the wrong that has been done to us, can take us far off course. And we're going to identify what rights we do have and how we can operate wisely in advocating for those we love and for ourselves.

## WHY DO PEOPLE DO HURTFUL THINGS?

As I've looked over the people in my life who have hurt me, whether the injury was deeply wounding or simply irritating like Mama Yeller was, here's what I've noticed: hurting people hurt people. I know it's a cliché, but it is so full of truth that it bears repeating: *hurting people hurt people*. They do. Just as a cornered animal with an injury will bare its teeth and growl, a hurting person will respond the same way, even if you're simply trying to help or just walking by.

Hurting people hurt others for a variety of reasons:

**Pain.** Hurting people often carry around a huge bag of unresolved pain slung over their shoulders. If they've experienced debilitating rejection in their lives, they will often respond by rejecting your best intentions, your invitation to connect. We often see this in those who have experienced sexual abuse. Many sexual-abuse survivors become some of the strongest advocates for protecting others and calling darkness into light. But there are also cases in which victims of childhood sexual abuse go on to become perpetrators. Sometimes an abusive parent was raised in a hurtful, anger-filled environment. It's been my experience that when people hurt others out of their own pain, they are seeking to alleviate the burden they carry or trying to protect themselves.

**Pride.** Some hurting people hurt others because, deep down, they really fear embarrassment. Some of the most vicious hurts I've had from people have stemmed from their place of pride. They know they're in the wrong, but they'll never admit it and never seek forgiveness out of their shame over their behavior. It would cost them too much to humble themselves, so instead they puff up, with arrogance and avarice as their shield.

**Jealousy.** Never underestimate the shards that can be spewed your way by a jealous spirit. Your gifting, your family, your achievements, your joy can all be targets for people who feel that if they haven't received their blessing, why should you enjoy yours? It's the person who can't celebrate your promotion and tells you you've gotten uppity ever since you got that new raise. It's the friend who tells you off, tells you you're not a good friend anymore, ever since you got involved in that romance you think might lead to marriage. These people don't know how to be happy for you. A jealous spirit can even fly at you from people you don't know. It's amazing to see some of the commentary flying around on social media or on message boards surrounding public figures. I myself have been a victim of this, with people who don't even know me making hurtful accusations about my lifestyle, my home, or my family. I'm very clear that the blessings in my life are because of God, not of my own making. But it's difficult for jealous people to rest in that. At the end of the day, they critique and jab and wound instead of seeking God's will and provision and blessing in their own lives.

**Entitlement**. There are plenty of people in the world who simply don't subscribe to the idea that they should love their neighbors as they love themselves. So they don't. They believe they should be able to elbow their way to the front of the line. They're the ones who zip by you on the shoulder of the highway while seemingly everyone else in town is stuck in traffic. They're the parents of fellow students in your child's class who nag and write nasty emails to get their kids the best, the most attention, the special treatment, regardless of the cost to other kids. People who hurt you out of a spirit of entitlement aren't taking something out on you personally; your feelings and thoughts and inconvenience or hurt don't even come to mind. Their agenda, their rights, their myopic view of the world is all they see.

**Lack of responsibility**. Sometimes people hurt us by gaslighting us. *Gaslight* is a term used frequently now, but the concept has been around a long time. It's when people, in an effort to manipulate you or not take responsibility for how they have hurt you, turn a situation around to make you question whether you're overreacting or your emotions are invalid or out of proportion. Of course, we are all capable of overreacting from time to time, and we have to stay mindful of that. But gaslighting is a pattern of behavior in which people seek to undermine the events in our relationship or our interactions with them and invalidate our experiences. These people act out of wanting to dodge their behavior, and they like to convince themselves that the injured party is a little crazy or oversensitive.

**Taking everything outward**. This reason for hurting others is similar to hurting from a sense of entitlement, but it comes from a different place. Hurting people may hurt others as they react to and process their own inner turmoil. They don't take a breath or pause to process. If they accidentally stub their toe, it's somehow your fault for not warning them. It's the gal who's had five jobs in five years and is about to get fired again but thinks her inability to keep a job has nothing to do with how she treats everyone in the office and the hurtful tone she uses in emails and on the phone. These kinds of people seem to bring their own tornadoes with them, shrapnel flying out in all directions, cutting anyone who happens to get in close proximity. And sometimes that happens to be you.

**Evil.** Okay, okay, I know it's not popular. We like to think that everyone has a little bit of good in them. But there are people in the history of the world who have abandoned themselves to the influence of the Enemy and have spewed ugliness. They maul, rage, steal, and pillage with abandon, with no pricking of the conscience, no acknowledgment of the emotions and rights of others. Adolf Hitler is an obvious example. You might have people in your life who have hurt you without remorse, without any indication they feel conflicted about their behavior. This is a category I don't throw around lightly. I can see woundedness even in the man who sexually abused me when I was a child, and I pray God's mercy over him. But there are those rare people in whom there seems to be no light, and they are often responsible for some of the cruelest things that happen to innocent people.

Where is God in all of this? We know from his Word that he is righteousness itself, that he embodies all that is good and just. He is also a loving Father who has extended to us an amazing freedom. He has given us the power of free will, the ability to choose. That remarkable gift carries with it a heavy responsibility. To choose wisely brings life. To choose poorly brings sin. And with sin comes the consequence of potentially hurting others.

Perhaps you've experienced the pain of people choosing to express their anger cruelly. Maybe you've experienced someone choosing to take your trust and crush it. I've been there. I've had trusted friends choose to turn against me and spread lies in very public ways. I've had an extended family member choose to make me a sexual-abuse victim. I've had people choose to steal from me.

But that's just it: the only solution for being hurt would be for God to remove from all of us the freedom he has extended. Where there is freedom, there will be sin, and sometimes that sin will be targeted at others. It's not fair. It makes me mad. It has often made me bring hard questions to God.

But at the end of the day, it has brought me a new respect for an important truth: sin is the enemy.

I've lost sight of this many times. I've made the people who have hurt me the enemy. But the truth is that it has been their sin, their choices that have hurt me. Although I have been the innocent party, reminding myself that sin is the enemy has allowed me to take a breath and look afresh at what it means for God to be my Defender. Because the deal is that I sin too. I don't like that fact. I don't like that I have this in common with those who have injured me, who have treated me poorly. I try to do my best to not allow my sin to spread its consequences on others. But there it is all the same. People who hurt me are sinners. People who love me well are sinners. And I'm a sinner too.

Which means there is only one Presence in my life who is qualified, who has the right, to act as judge.

Jehovah El Elyon. My Defender. My Rock. My Refuge. My Strength.

It has taken many years for me to learn this well. There were years when I refused to reveal the abuse in my life, thinking that avoiding the truth could somehow make the pain less true. By not bringing that darkness into the light, I wasn't letting God be my Defender, but rather, I was relying on my silence to protect me. Then there were years when I decided I would never be taken advantage of again, and I would rage and plot and fight openly against those I felt were exploiting me. I can tell you that revenge can taste sweet when you've spent previous years feeling helpless. But that doesn't make it right.

I've also lengthened my journey toward healing by getting stuck on the very questions that may be keeping you stuck as well.

Why do bad things happen? We won't come up with an answer that will satisfy.

Why do people do bad things? Because sin is the enemy.

Am I going to let evil win in me? No.

So here are my questions to you: What do you think about allowing God to be your Defender? Are you ready to find peace in the midst of hurt? Are you ready to find true restoration?

Are you ready?

Then let's begin.

*one*

# THE TRUE BATTLE

I'M CURRENTLY NOT FEEDING MY HUSBAND.

I have good reason, the way I think about it. It's because of the garage.

I'm sure this makes perfect sense to you, but let me explain.

We have just come out of an extensive season of home renovation. If you've been through a home renovation, you know about setbacks and stress. Everything takes longer than you thought it would. It's all much more expensive than you planned. It's weeks of knowing that if only the plumber would show up like he said he would, then you could wrap this whole thing up. But the plumber has gone MIA, which means the electrician has to be canceled, and he doesn't have an opening again until the middle of next month. Which of course means you'll have to delay the delivery of the cabinets because, you guessed it, the electrical has to be in place in order to install the cabinets, and the electrical can't be done until the missing plumber decides to grace your home reno with his presence. It all makes me think of that children's book *If You Give a Mouse a Cookie*, in which a whole series of events goes down like dominoes, leading to lighthearted catastrophe, all because a rodent received a pastry. In my mind, the grown-up version of this book would be *If You Give a Plumber a Check*, with less lighthearted results.

I'm someone who does better when I inhabit a space that is orderly and put together. I can focus; I can relax. When my environment, whether home or office, is upside down, my attitude can get a little, say, testy—and this reno had outstayed its welcome.

It had been months of navigating the upside down, and I was more than ready to live in our home in a way that didn't feel like camping out in a home improvement store.

The plumber finally did show up, then the electrician, then the cabinets. The house looks amazing, and I'm happy with how it all turned out, even if the timeline fell apart. There's just one little nagging thing that remains.

The garage.

The garage is a disaster. Crates and supplies and paint drop cloths and all kinds of household sediment that don't really have a place in the fresh new reno but that we're still hanging on to. The dusty chemical smell of old paint and musty sawdust and dingy cardboard boxes hangs like a haze. When I pull up to the house after a long day, that garage situation greets me like a pimple on the end of a nose. I can't unsee it. It's all I see.

My husband is supposed to take care of the garage situation, and he hasn't done it. He assured me he would, but it's been several weeks now, and I've reminded, asked, used polite terms. It still hasn't been done.

So I've taken charge of the situation. If you think that means I've had a frank, direct conversation with my husband or hired a cleaning crew or asked my husband how I can help, you'd be wrong.

No, no, no.

The kind of charge I've taken is refusing to cook for him.

It started with not making his favorite meal for a couple of weeks in a row. Now I've let it grow to not cooking in a general way, favorite meal or not. I'm doing it for his own good, you understand. By not cooking for him, I'm helping to teach him about not getting that garage cleaned out.

Iron sharpening iron, baby.

I try to tell myself that I'm not punishing him. I try to justify my behavior as teaching him a lesson. But even just saying these thoughts out loud to myself reveals what's really going on in my heart.

I'm taking revenge. Over a messy garage.

Lord, help.

This sweet husband of mine—the guy who worships with all his heart, the man who is supportive of my dreams, the dreamboat willing to play Barbies with our daughter—is the one I'm taking vengeance on. It's important to mention here that he was the person who oversaw all of the renovation, managed the details, and handled the twists and turns and frustrations that a home project of this magnitude brings. He didn't do it only for our family; he generously oversaw home reno projects for some of our extended family members too. He's done all this. But it's the garage I see.

So I withhold something he loves in our dynamic, something he loves about me: my skills as a chef for our family. The sweetness of sitting down together at the end of the day and reconnecting over delicious food and laughter and conversation.

Makes perfect sense, right? Not.

Let's have a moment of quiet confession time together, just you and me. You do this too, right? Someone frustrates you or sends you an email that has that tone to it or forgets to handle a detail they promised they would, so you come up with a way to create a tiny gap between the two of you. You think up a little something to give them a lesson. That old classic, the silent treatment. That new classic, the blistering online review. The withdrawn invitation. Leaving a text message unread.

I justify these responses as putting up boundaries, but a healthy boundary doesn't look like some of the means I employ. And, no judgment here, but I bet you justify some of your responses the same way.

Hey, we're all friends here. We're in this together. I'm working on my heart, and you're working on yours. If we're going to lean into letting God be our Defender, then we've got to come clean on whom the real battle is with when it comes to letting God be God.

The real battle is with ourselves.

Our sense of right and wrong. Our sense of fair. Our sense of timing. Our personalities. The baggage we carry from previous experiences. These all have an impact on our ability and willingness to allow God to defend us instead of jumping into the fray with retribution in our hearts and sharp words on our tongues—or shoving those hurts under the rug for no one to see.

And this is just our response to what we'd call the small stuff, the little things that are done to us (or not done, as is the case with my garage). When big stuff comes our way, it's even harder for most of us not to respond with bigger expressions of retaliation. That's why I say that the true battle when it comes to the ways we are wronged in life is with ourselves. We can't control how people around us are going to treat us. We can't control their reactions, their nagging, or their neglect. The only person in the equation that we get to make behavior choices for is us.

When I zoom out and look at some of my bigger wounds, I'm struck by this one truth: my response is the only thing I can control. There have been hurts I've handled with honesty and grace. And there have been times I've been gunning for full-out revenge.

Okay, okay, full-out revenge might seem a little dramatic. Sometimes I hold a grudge and tell myself it's just a little one. But grudges are a form of retaliation. Have you ever stopped to think about that? Sometimes I want to excuse my response to a hurt by minimizing my reaction. "Just" a grudge. "Just" a little silent treatment. "Just" a little gossip session to inform someone who needs to know about the behavior of another.

But anytime I take matters into my own hands without first taking them to God, I'm at risk of violating these important words: "Do not seek revenge or bear a grudge against anyone among your people, but love your neighbor as yourself. I am the LORD" (Lev. 19:18).

Does that mean that I never speak up, never confront, never ask to speak to a manager? Nope. Of course not. What it does mean is that I must first seek God's cleansing of my own heart so that in my anger or my hurt or my confusion or my sense of rejection or violation, I don't respond in sin. Just as two wrongs don't make a right, neither does a sin met with a sin correct a situation.

To be able to acknowledge God as your Defender and to be able to hear his leading in dealing with hurtful situations, it's helpful to think about the kind of "first-responder" personality you have in situations when you are wronged. For me, being clear about who I am helps me understand and refine my reactions in difficult environments. See if you can find yourself in the following descriptions of first responders.

## TEACHER

I'm a teacher. That's one of the things God has gifted me to do. It's a calling I take on with awe and, I hope, a great deal of humility. But I can also turn that gift into thinking it's my right to teach people a lesson. That may be your story too. You may be a teacher by vocation, or it may be something in your marrow, that thing you always seem to be doing, whether in a classroom, on a stage, or in the grocery store baking aisle, helping a stranger understand the difference between baking soda and baking powder.

It's hard for me to turn off the teaching thing when it comes to irritations, big and small, that make their way into my day. When people do something wrong, I just itch with the need to set it straight, to help them see the error of their ways and get back on the right path. Which sometimes leads me to hold grudges over things like dirty garages and meals for my husband. Sigh.

I don't need to teach my husband a lesson. I need to have a conversation with him. We're adults. He's not my student. And that's the challenge for those of us who identify as teachers: not everyone is our student. My battle is to be honest about the difference between using my teaching gift in the way God intends and using it for "teaching" a grudge.

## ADVOCATE

Is this you? You have no problem letting a waiter know when your order is wrong. You're more than happy to stand up at a PTA meeting and call out the problems with the students' new lunchtime schedule. You're not necessarily looking to pick a fight, but you're ready to lead the charge when it comes to the things you see as inequitable or unfair. You're ready to charge the hill, call the news, put out the petition, post the review. You're wired as a protector, and that's a beautiful thing. But all that gifting God placed in you has to be submitted first to him.

Do you stop and pray before you act? Or are you zero to

seventy in a hot minute? Do you check your tone and your approach against that handy list of the fruit of the Spirit in Galatians? Do you exhibit love, joy, peace, *patience*, kindness, goodness, faithfulness, *gentleness*, and *self-control*? (The ones in italics are the ones I'm wondering about.) As an advocate, you can be a powerful force for good when you stand behind God as your Defender, when you let him lead. But when you get out ahead of him, things can go sideways fast. It can be easy not to see the impact your well-meaning protectiveness can have on others.

Advocates can also struggle with *proportion*. Let's say hurts in life have a "volume," if you will, and let's say a hurt comes along that is a four out of ten on that volume scale. I've seen advocates come in at a ten in response, simply out of their passion to set things right. When we are leaning on God as our Defender, it's critical to keep an accurate understanding of the scope of the issue—its volume—so that we can hear his leading and not the roaring of our own inner dialogue.

## LOYALIST

You may not stand up for yourself all that often. You think you can take a lot, and you do try to turn the other cheek. You don't involve yourself in a lot of causes; you don't feel the need to rant about some controversy or other on social media. But if someone crosses one of your people, all bets are off. You may have even referred to yourself as a "mama bear."

We are supposed to defend the cause of those who are being compromised. We are supposed to stand up to bullies and protect those who cannot protect themselves. But it's a delicate balance. Sometimes our loyalty can render us incapable of recognizing that maybe, just maybe, our innocent little darling actually *did* instigate that squabble with the other kid in her class. It can make us choose sides and turn a blind eye to the other side of the story. When we go rushing in from the position of a loyalist, particularly when we don't have all the facts, we unintentionally do more harm.

God values loyalty. But our loyalty must be to him first. When our loyalty lies first with our family, our kids, or our friends, and we justify aggressive behavior as a sign of that loyalty, we show that we are more concerned with pleasing our people than we are with pleasing our God.

## SILENT SUFFERER

You've been wronged—badly so. Maybe the wrong has come in a consistent, insidious way from someone close to you, and you have a hard time recognizing it for what it is: a form of emotional abuse that compounds. Maybe you've been flagrantly hurt. But you keep silent—because isn't that what a good Christian does? Underneath the silence, underneath the secrets, a storm is brewing. Perhaps you don't speak up because you're scared; maybe you've even been threatened if you come forward with the truth. But your fear has become bigger than your God, and that means that your reliance is on the quiet you keep, not on the Defender who longs to free you. It's time to seek the counsel that will allow you to speak the truth. It's going to take work, and it's going to take courage. God will meet you there.

When the Israelites were about to go into the promised land, they were terrified. Moses was getting ready to step down as their leader, and Joshua was about to take up the post. The Israelites had heard there were giants in the land. But Moses proclaimed these gorgeous words over them: "Be strong and courageous. Do not be afraid or terrified because of them, for the LORD your God goes with you; he will never leave you nor forsake you" (Deut. 31:6). As your Defender, God goes ahead of you into the unknown. Is it terrifying to disclose a truth about a hurt you've never discussed before? Of course. But God goes with you into that unknown terrain. The truth sets you free and reveals God's protection on your behalf.

## THE COMPANY YOU KEEP

What first-responder style did you discover is your go-to? It's so helpful to identify what response is the most common for you. It will help you see it in yourself in hurtful situations and help you frame better responses and healthier perspectives. But it's not just our personal approaches to how we deal with hurt that define our experiences. Other factors that play a role are the people we surround ourselves with and how we experience upsetting events.

Here's a weird thing about our reactions to being hurt: it's often in some of our closest relationships that we exact our more petty forms of revenge. I've had other wives tell me, with no embarrassment or remorse, that they withhold sex when their husbands have done something to tick them off. I'm always a little surprised by this, until the Holy Spirit reminds me that I'm currently withholding home cooking from mine. I'm not pointing fingers here; I'm just referencing that we all have our little ways of emphasizing to those we're closest to how we've been injured.

Here's another weird thing: those on the outside of our inner circle may be the ones we aren't as honest with about our hurts. That extended family member who has never thanked you for bailing him out of a bad situation? You may keep quiet. That coworker who routinely makes you feel minimized in meetings? Yep. You see the conflict underneath, but you keep peace in the office.

And here's one more weird thing: it's sometimes people we don't know at all who get the full brunt of our biggest reactions to frustrations and hurts. Have you noticed this? The anonymous customer service person on the other end of the phone who monotonously tells you she can't help you with the inaccurate, exorbitant charge on your cell phone bill? You'll verbally light her up like a Christmas tree with language you'd never use with a friend. That guy in the parking lot who zipped into the space you were clearly signaling for? In two beats, you find yourself throwing your car into park in the middle of the row and marching over to blast him for his ungentlemanly behavior.

What is happening in those moments? We have to be vigilant to watch ourselves when there seems to be no long-term risk in voicing how we were wronged to people we don't know and will probably never encounter again. The guardrails that may keep us safe in closer relationships sometimes come down with people we don't know, and we can find ourselves reacting far outside of what is helpful, what is good, what is of God. Now listen: I follow a Jesus who, yes, knew how to flip money changers' tables in the temple courtyard. He wasn't afraid to make some noise when it was needed. But it was always, always subject to his Father. It was always under the precepts of God. There were times Jesus stood up—but he also knew when to stand down. Knowing the difference, knowing which time is which, is knowing that God is your Defender.

# NOT EVERY HURT HAS TO HURT

Here's another part of the true battle that is tricky: just because something stings you, it doesn't mean you need defending. Read that again. Not every hurt from someone has to wound. Sometimes it can wind up making you better.

I was on a particular reality-TV show a few years ago. Regardless of your opinion of reality TV, it is a fascinating lab of human emotion and interaction. When I started the show, I didn't really know many of my costars. All the women on the show were in the process of developing friendships—or frenemy-ships, in some cases. When I joined the show, the producers kept the cameras rolling as my castmates and I sat down over wine and crackers to get to know each other better.

I don't usually drink wine, and I was pretty much the one person really working my way through the crackers. They were good! I was chatting with all the women, these new costars of mine, getting to know them, hearing their stories. One of the women, watching me crunch through the crackers, turned to me and said, "You know, Rosie, if you were a little thinner, you'd be even more beautiful!"

I was shocked. The conversation on set came to a complete halt. But the cameras kept rolling. Everyone was waiting to see how I was going to react.

The sassy part of me recovered first. I looked her straight in the face, grabbed another cracker, and shoved it in my mouth. I'm here to tell you, that spite cracker tasted better than all the rest.

Laughter followed, and the situation was defused.

But inside, her comment stung. While her words might have seemed harsh or insensitive, I don't think her remark was personal; it was more about getting camera time. And the truth was that I had let my eating habits get away from me quite a bit. Now, I'm not here to make anyone feel bad about their bodies or about what the scale says. I just know there are times when I'm not living in a healthy manner when it comes to my relationship with food, and that's where I was during those early days on that show. I was quite a bit heavier than is healthy for me.

So.

I could have resented the comment my costar made. And please know, it did hurt.

But I had a decision to make. Was I going to let it hurt my relationship with her? Was I going to verbally blast her with a zinger, cameras rolling, the next time I was with her? Or was I going to let that hurt minister to me and make me better?

By God's grace, I chose the better way. God as my Defender means he's always seeking what is best for me. And in this case, getting a better hold on my health and my habits was the best defense he could have offered.

So I took him up on it. God gave me the tenacity to start jogging. It was rough at first, but I kept at it. He gave me the spirit of self-discipline through his Holy Spirit, and I began eating in a way that was better for my body. Over the course of the next few months, the weight came off, both in body and heaviness of heart.

Here's the point: I could have easily lost the battle on this one. I could have taken my costar's words and stirred them up into a furious froth. I could have nursed that hurt with more unhealthy eating habits. I could have decided that my fight was with her instead of with the truth that I was letting my health get out of control.

Not every hurt has to hurt, at least not in the way we often take it. Sometimes we receive a truth we don't want to hear, and we make the messenger the bad guy. I love this verse from

Proverbs: "A person's wisdom yields patience; it is to one's glory to overlook an offense" (19:11). Look, sometimes what people say to you may offend you because of the way they do it. It may offend you because of how they handle it. But it just may be that they are actually pointing out something that can be for your good. If we're going to let God be our Defender, we have to become discerning and mature about understanding the difference between someone unfairly hurting us and someone who simply has style issues.

As we continue on this journey together and uncover the ways God acts as our Defender, as we identify the pitfalls and distractions that can keep us from fully experiencing his love and protection, let's take the time to think through the battle with ourselves.

Read this prayer out loud:

*Father God,*

*You know the hurts I have faced in life. You know the secret ones I've never talked about. You know the ones I'm facing today. You know how you knit me together, and you know the way I want to respond to these inequities, as well as the ways I've responded in the past.*

*Father, I ask you to give me fresh eyes to see where I may be operating out of a grudge, out of a spirit of revenge. I ask you to give me fresh eyes to see where I may be operating out of fear. I ask you to give me fresh eyes to see where I may be responding in opposition to your will.*

*Father, remind me that you are with me. Remind me that you are my Rock, my Fortress, and my Shield. Help me fight well the battle that is the most important one: the battle with myself. The battle with my fears, my wounds, my past, my anger. Thank you that you call me beloved. Thank you that you are always moving on my behalf, including moving within my own heart and spirit to make me more like you.*

*In the name of Jesus, amen.*

All right, my friend. Before we dive into the next chapter, I guess it's time for me to go make dinner and quit serving up a cold dish of revenge.

# *two*
# GOING ON THE JOURNEY

I'VE SPENT A LOT OF TIME IN THE PEPPERMINT FOREST.

You may be thinking, *Where on earth is the Peppermint Forest, and why has Rosie spent a lot of time there? Is that somewhere up in the Canadian Rockies?*

Not that I'm aware of. No, the Peppermint Forest exists in the wilds of motherhood. It's the place where I seem to get stuck time and time again in the classic children's board game Candy Land.

The game of Candy Land has been a bestseller ever since it was first offered on the market, and it has a really cool backstory: It was developed by Eleanor Abbott, a retired schoolteacher who was recovering from polio in a hospital ward in San Diego, California. She saw how lonely the children in the ward were and wanted them to have a game to keep them engaged, one that wasn't too complicated but would keep their attention. Even today, more than a million units of Candy Land are sold every year.[1] That's some serious staying power in a culture that's always about newer, bigger, and better.

The purpose of the game is simple: you draw a card and move your playing piece according to what's on that card, trying to get to the end of the game board as quickly as possible. But as any tired mom of a preschooler trying to get through this game will tell you, there are dangers in that card deck. Just when you think you've wrapped up the game, you'll draw one of those cards that sends you all the way back through the Molasses Swamp, over the Gumdrop Mountains, past the Peppermint Forest to the beginning.

I love being a mom, but playing Candy Land is one of those mom things I have to question the sanity of. (I'm sorry, Ms. Abbott.) Yes, it's a classic. Yes, it helps teach kids how games work and about colors and counting. Yes, it counts as quality time with the kids. Sure, it's cute and has a retro vibe. But good heavens, how many times can you get stuck in the Peppermint Forest and not start losing your cool?

The funny thing is, the game rules say that if you have a young child who would get frustrated and teary being sent back to the beginning of the board, you may skip that rule and simply progress toward the Candy Castle, the ultimate destination and goal of each player. But would my kids allow that faster kind of game to be played?

Nope.

They wanted to play it with all legalism intact, so classic style we played. But my inner dialogue each time I got sent back to the beginning was surely that of a cranky toddler in need of a snack and a nap.

Turns out, Candy Land is a good metaphor for how some of my spiritual life works, too, particularly when it comes to vindication for the wrongs I've experienced at the hands of others. I'll be making progress in my journey, feeling like I'm edging my way toward forgiveness, toward freedom. But then I'll draw a card in the form of a trigger, a passing phrase, an old memory, a photograph of when I was a young teenager, and all the shame will come rushing back. The progress I've made will disappear, and I'll find myself back at the beginning of the board, processing some of the same emotions and hurt and need for revenge that I thought I'd left behind.

In the journey toward freedom, the itch for revenge is the card that sends you back to the beginning of the board.

# WHEN THE JOURNEY BEGINS

Whatever wrong, hurt, or injustice I face, that initial experience marks the start of a journey toward a place where I rest fully in having God as my Defender. It's a journey with lots of ups and downs. It's a journey in which I have to face some uncomfortable truths about myself. It's a journey that usually goes on a lot longer than I would like. On this journey, I sometimes move a couple of steps forward and then go sliding way back—back to emotions I'd rather leave behind, back to questions that don't help, back to relying on my own methods of defending myself instead of God's.

I used to think that moving beyond the harms and wrongs in my life was a one-time, one-stop experience. I dreamed there would be a moment when I would see the abuser get what was coming to him. I looked for a time when people who had lied about me or used my sister's fame or said something mean about one of my kids would experience retribution. I thought if I could see that happen, I would be healed.

I'm sure there are times when people get to have that kind of closure, when all the wrongs and hurts get resolved and packed up into a tidy box, complete with a lock that defies any kind of break-in. But that has not been the case for me. It's been the long game, a journey, a series of victories and setbacks. I used to think this was a failure on my part.

Perhaps if I just prayed more, I would see things set right faster. Maybe if I were more generous in several areas of my life, the payback would show up. Maybe if I . . . maybe if I . . . maybe if I. I used to trade "good behavior" for God's love and favor, something I've done in other relationships as well. I've had a whole series of if-then bargains in my head, things I thought I could exchange for a guarantee that I would find a resolution to some of the open-ended situations I've faced.

Have you tried to bargain your way out of the journey? Have you created elaborate scenarios in your head where, in front of a spellbound crowd, you get to tell off the person who wronged you, a la any courtroom drama you've ever seen? Do you offer up a certain behavior or approach in the hopes that it will lead to closure?

I'm ready to close the chapter. I don't want it to be a long read or a long road. But then I find this in God's Word:

> It was for me the day of vengeance;
>     the year for me to redeem had come. (Isa. 63:4)

If I'm reading this correctly, for a lot of things we want to see God make right, he may have another day, another year for that to come to pass. It won't happen on our preferred, more immediate schedule.

Which means that you and I are on a journey. I want to make forward progress. I don't want to get sent back to the beginning of my emotional Candy Land board, slipping and sliding backward into the sharp teeth of hurt and rage and bitterness. How do we do it? How do we navigate the journey with vibrancy and hope instead of slipping back—or staying strapped—to the original situation?

# DOWNHILL

My husband, Abel, and I set out on a journey a few years ago. It was winter, and we left our sunny home base of Southern

California to head to the cold of Buena Vista, Colorado, a small town just below soaring Mount Princeton in the Rockies. I would love to tell you that we were headed to such a gorgeous place for the skiing, with plans to do some serious downhill runs.

Well, there was a serious downhill run going on. But it wasn't on skis.

Our marriage was in trouble, heading downhill fast, with what seemed like an inevitable wipeout on the horizon. We hadn't even been married all that long—only six months. But the problems and fights and tears were multiplying by the day, and our issues seemed to be accelerating more and more quickly, snowballing as the challenges kept coming. We decided we needed to do something, so there we were, locked in a car together for fifteen hours as we crossed the high deserts of California and Nevada, the salt flats of Utah, and the western edges of Colorado—headed toward what just might be a last-ditch effort at salvaging our relationship.

There was a marriage-counseling group in Buena Vista that our pastor had recommended we seek out. So Abel and I made the arrangements, figured out the budget, packed our suitcases in silent rage, and began the trek. We were driving instead of flying because money was supertight, and it was the only way we could make the counseling tab and the travel work.

Let me tell you something: having to drive a third of the way across the country with someone you're needing to do an emergency counseling deep dive with is, um, awkward. Difficult.

Weird, actually.

The drive we were making is truly beautiful. The high deserts of California and Nevada are awash in stunning shades of neutrals and reds and corals, and the sky is the deepest blue you'll ever see. Hours and hours later, when we crossed the state line into southern Utah, it was into some of the most dramatic, glorious landscapes I had ever seen. Red cliffs, valleys carved of stone, towers of rock. Then Salt Lake Valley itself, with Great Salt Lake and the soaring Wasatch Range—well, it's some of the most incredible scenery you can imagine.

I'd love to tell you that I took it all in, that in seeing this powerful display of God's power and creativity and beauty, our hearts were softened, and the miles rolling beneath our tires brought us closer to each other.

But that would be a big no. With a capital *N*.

That trip out to Colorado was filled with so much anger. I couldn't really take in the scenery. I couldn't really see the majesty of what was right outside my car window. I was too focused on not speaking to Abel. I was too focused on the pinpoints of my hurt. I was too focused on everything that was wrong to be able to see what was right in the world: mountains, sky, colors, quiet. At a dusty truck stop along the way, we finally decided to at least look at the remainder of the road trip as a kind of adventure. We're not friends, we decided, but let's try not to be enemies. We called a cease-fire so we could at least talk about neutral topics as the day gave way to darkness and we still had several hours to drive.

When we finally arrived in Buena Vista, we found a beautiful cabin awaiting us. We lugged our suitcases in and tried to get some sleep, each of us rigidly turned away from each other, glued to our separate sides of the bed. Exhausted as I was, my frustration burned like a furnace in my heart and head, keeping me awake for hours, fueled by indignation and ghosts.

See, that was one of the craziest parts about the situation between Abel and me. Yes, there were problems between the two of us that needed work. But a lot of what was going on was about external family issues and conflict—and my challenges as a sexual-abuse survivor. While I had really healed spiritually, I had some serious mommy issues rattling through my heart. I had thought that my marriage with Abel would be a new start, a fresh page. Instead, just like in that crazy game of Candy Land, after what I thought was solid progress, I now found myself sliding backward, slipping back into emotions and memories I thought I had moved beyond. Little things Abel did irritated me or brought up uncomfortable memories that would send me into overdrive. Ghosts of hurts past roared to life in this new love, in this new life, repeating old songs and old patterns.

We started intensive counseling sessions the next morning. The counselors were great, the accommodations lovely, everything crafted to give us the best chance to make changes in our marriage and the tools and guidance to heal. I would love to tell you it worked. All the right ingredients were there, and we were given all the love and counsel and wisdom we could ever hope for. If any place could have worked, it should have been this one.

It didn't.

It didn't work at all.

Please hear me: it wasn't because of the practice. All of that was spot-on, and if you're ever able to go there, do it. I know it can change things for you.

But here's why it didn't work for us. One simple little thing.

Me.

I wasn't ready to receive their help. What I wanted was to vent. I didn't want tools; I wanted to tangle. I didn't want peace; I wanted to emotionally punch. I didn't want to heal; I wanted to reexamine every hurt. I wanted to relive everything that had been done to me.

I wasn't ready to move down the board. I wasn't ready to leave the Peppermint Forest behind.

We did all the right things: attended the sessions, filled out the journals, had the stilted conversations in front of the counselor. But we also ate our meals in stony silence, took hostile walks around the property, and gazed at the mountains through red-rimmed eyes. Then our multiday stay was over, and it was time for us to leave and slide back down the map to LA Land, back to the patterns that had led us there, back to the repeated scripts of old hurts and fresh triggers and seeming hopelessness.

We packed our bags while blankets of snow fell outside, turning the fields around the retreat center sparkling white. We threw everything into the back of our Prius, said our goodbyes to our concerned counselor and staff, and made our way gingerly back across the mountains. The road was narrow, with a steep cliff to our left and snow falling heavily. We were about an hour into the journey when I realized I had forgotten some medicine back at the cabin. We decided to turn around and go back to get it. Abel found a spot to make a U-turn on the narrow, snow-covered road and carefully began to make the turn.

That's when it happened.

The tires lost their grip on the slippery asphalt, and the back tires spun. We were rolling down the cliff. Somehow, miraculously, the car came to a halt before it fell all the way to the bottom of the ravine.

Hearts pounding, our breath coming in frantic gasps, Abel and I stared at each other, stunned at what had happened and also shocked that we were okay, that we weren't scattered in pieces across the bottom of the icy ravine. We should have been dead. But we weren't.

We were able to get the car started and out of the ravine. Then we resumed our long trek home, silence our only music and conversation.

But this was a different kind of silence than the one we'd had on our way to Buena Vista. That silence had been the kind filled with upset and unspoken battles. This silence was the kind filled with pondering. With wonder. With listening and processing.

Somewhere around Las Vegas, I turned on the song "The House That Built Me," recorded by country music star Miranda Lambert and written by Tom Douglas and Allen Shamblin. If you haven't heard the song, take a break and listen to it. And be sure to look up the lyrics. That song just gets me, and on this long trip home, it cracked me wide open. I started crying and crying. Abel asked me to talk, to tell him all that was on my heart. So I did. I talked through the things that had happened to me, the stories he knew of the sexual abuse I had endured, of my tumultuous teenage years and unhealthy relationships, of the emotions that resulted. Yes, he already knew of those occurrences, but now he listened with a different intent. He listened not just to understand what had happened to me and how it had shaped me, but to understand *me*. As he listened, I came to a startling realization: under so much of the anger I was feeling toward him was pain that had nothing to do with him.

You see, in that tumble into the mouth of the ravine, we were scared. Deeply, crazy, wet-your-pants kind of scared. That kind of fear can wake you up, make you really think about where you've been targeting your anger. In the silence that followed, we both realized the same thing: maybe we did want each other. How would it have felt if one of us had lost the other in the midst of that marriage war? Would holding on to the anger and resentment have been worth it?

This thought kept resounding in my heart and head: *I don't want us to die before we physically die.* Since I knew that to be true, it was time to answer this question: Is the war going to continue, or is it time to play through? Time to not allow myself to get pulled back to places I'd already been, feeling emotions I'd gone over time and again, emotions I was now directing at my husband. Time to take steps of progression instead of regression. What if?

That marriage 911 trip? Well, we didn't come home fixed. It wasn't the solution to everything that was haunting us. But something shifted—and sometimes, shifting can make all the difference.

## WHAT PATH ARE YOU ON?

Believe me, I didn't set out to keep revisiting the wrongs done to me. It wasn't as if I hadn't gotten a good enough look the first time. But here's the thing about the traumas and injuries we suffer: Modern science tells us that everything we experience creates pathways in our brains. If you have something good, something pleasurable, happen to you, it creates a pathway that's reinforced each time you experience it. So if you got praise as a kid for getting a good grade on your spelling test, you're more likely to want to work to get a good grade the next time too. How you've been hurt in your life has also laid down a pathway. Anytime something similar to that original hurt comes along, whether it's a tone of voice or a certain scent or simply feeling scared or insecure, it can send your mind and heart tumbling down that old path, feeling the same things, awakening pain.

The Word of God has all kinds of verses about paths—good paths, bad paths, narrow ones, and wide ones. We love to quote verses like "Your word is a lamp for my feet, a light on my path" (Ps. 119:105). But it's also important to look at verses that talk about the dangers of certain paths and how we can end up going down them if we're not on watch. Some of those paths have to do with our own sin natures, when we choose unrighteous behavior instead of God's best. Job 22:15 says, "Will you keep to the old path that the wicked have trod?" (I do love that this path of the wicked is referred to as "old." We like to think that we've come up with "modern" ways to sin, that we're creative in how we turn away from the Lord. But wicked is wicked, no matter the century, am I right?)

But there's another kind of path we move down in our lives, and it has its own dangers. King David said it this way: "Teach me your way, LORD; lead me in a straight path because of my oppressors. Do not turn me over to the desire of my foes" (Ps. 27:11–12). What this says to me is that if I'm not careful to walk in righteousness when it comes to dealing with the hurts in my life and the way I want to see others brought to justice for what they've done, I could put myself in danger of wandering off God's path and back into the same loop I'm trying so desperately to escape.

As you might know, there are many translations of the Bible, and I like to take a look at verses in several different ones. Why are there different translations? Well, the Bible was originally written down in Hebrew in the Old Testament, and in an ancient form of Greek in the New Testament. Just as in my native tongue, Spanish, there are words or phrases in those languages that have several equivalent words in English. So it helps me to look at a couple more translations to get the full idea of what the Bible is saying. (You can look up several translations easily on websites like www.biblegateway.com.) When it comes to Psalm 27, I like the Living Bible translation as well:

> Tell me what to do, O Lord, and make it plain because I am surrounded by waiting enemies. Don't let them get me, Lord! Don't let me fall into their hands! For they accuse me of things I never did, and all the while are plotting cruelty. (vv. 11–12)

Our oppressor is Satan, and he loves to keep us from moving forward.

I've bought into his ploy more times than I'd like to admit. Part of the "logic" the Enemy tries to lay on us is that getting revenge will "fix" things. But revenge is a spiral that takes us all the way to the pit. When I wasn't getting revenge on those who had abused me, I shifted my attack to my husband. It makes me think about a guy in the Bible named Jephthah. His story is in the Old Testament book of Judges, in chapter 11. He wanted revenge against the Ammonites, who were threatening the borders of his land and had been taking over certain portions of his family's territory. He went out to battle them and told God that if he won, he would sacrifice the first living creature that came out his front door to welcome him home. Vowing something like that sounds crazy to us, but it's what he did.

Jephthah battled his enemies. He wiped out several of their towns and took back everything he felt they had stolen from him. But when he arrived home, the very first person to come out his front door to congratulate him was his only daughter.

Jephthah ended up sacrificing her to keep his vow.

This sounds superextreme, right? But that's the danger of promising anything in exchange for revenge. Sure, Jephthah gained back his land, but what he sacrificed was something of far greater worth. That's the problem with putting a timeline on vindication and hanging on tightly to the emotions and indignation and rage that result when our territory has been invaded: it can cost us what is most important. I was at risk of doing this with my marriage. In trying to find an outlet for what had been done to me, I was often willing to sacrifice the first one to greet me when I arrived home: my husband.

Here's what I'm figuring out in this revenge game: you don't want to have to go back to the beginning of the board.

How do you avoid that? How do you be honest about what has happened to you, be real about your emotions, but not get caught in some weird loop where you seem to be reliving it over and over?

As we travel together through this book, through the Spiral of Fair, the Isles of Idolatry, the Quicksand of Self-Destruction, and many other places along the way, remember that relationship, specifically our relationship with God, is the point of the journey. It's a mission of discovering his place as our Defender. So be honest with yourself. Is revenge your highest priority? Or is God? Wherever you land today is okay, but keep reading. I pray that relationship with your Father becomes your chief aim.

We're going to take a look at some different journeys people have set out on, all of them in an attempt to find closure. Some of them get turned around. Some of them slide back. All of them teach us important truths about the slippery path of revenge and how to find solid footing that leads to a healed and abundant life.

## BEFORE WE MOVE ON

*Here are some important questions to ask yourself as you begin
your journey toward healing:*

1.  Do you know what your triggers are? Listen, girl, this is really
    important. Lean in. A trigger is anything that takes you right back
    to the abuse, the fear, the pain. For the husband who cheated on
    you and left, it could be the song that was "your" song. For the
    boss who was toxic and cut you down at every turn, it could be
    the verbiage that she used. It could be a location that looks like
    the place that guy cornered you and made unwanted advances.
    It could even be a verse that your pastor used to justify being
    overly controlling. Whatever it is for you, do you know it? Do you
    recognize it? Pay attention to how it affects you. Journal about it.
    Bring it forward into your mind and recognize it. Ephesians 5:13
    says, "Everything exposed by the light becomes visible—and
    everything that is illuminated becomes a light." So bring those
    triggers into the light and see them for what they are.

2.  Have you communicated those triggers to the people closest
    to you? Abel knew my story, but I also needed to equip him
    to understand how certain things could inadvertently set me
    off. Let me make this clear: I have a responsibility to work
    with the Lord to begin unraveling the power some of these
    triggers have over me, so it's not Abel's duty to constantly
    be on "trigger guard." But it's helpful for those close to you
    to understand how your past hurts, particularly those that
    remain unresolved, play into how you experience things
    and how seemingly harmless comments can lead to big
    throw-downs.

3.  What is most important to you, revenge or relationship? I'm not suggesting you go back to an abuser or put a relationship over a deeply toxic or dangerous situation. There are going to be people it would be unwise for you to have a relationship with moving forward. But sometimes we get so focused on revenge that we forget that relationship is the goal. If revenge is the point of the journey, the journey is pointless. Make it your goal to find your way to God as you make this journey of justice.

*three*

# THE SPIRAL OF FAIR

## "IT'S NOT FAIR!"

Cue the stomping up the stairs. Cue the dramatic sigh. Cue the door slamming.

Since I'm a mom of three kids, you're probably thinking that the above script is a pretty common occurrence around our house. You would be right.

But now I have to confess: That tear-filled cry of "It's not fair!"? That dramatic sigh? That door slamming?

Well, it comes from me, but now as an adult, I've learned to slam the door on the inside.

We talked earlier about how your personality style plays into your journey when it comes to how you want to see things made right. I've already shared with you that I'm a teacher at heart, and I can use that teaching gift as a tool for wielding a grudge. There's something else I've learned about myself, and this might be true for you too: I seem to have come wired with a really strong sense of justice. I really thought I would be a lawyer one day. I love to study court cases. I love to review contracts. I've done a lot of reading on the subject, and of course, there are all those legal dramas on TV that have been part of my education as well. There is a satisfaction like no other for me when I see the bad guy caught, when I find the hidden clause in the contract that makes things equitable, when that which was wrong is reset to right— and it all has to do with the idea of what is fair.

I grew up with a lot of siblings, so you better believe we were always looking for things to be fair. My sister and brothers and I were always keeping an eye out for who had to work the stand at the flea market (not fair!), who got to go fruit picking with Dad out in Fresno (not fair!), who got the new pair of jeans versus who got the hand-me-downs (not fair!). The phrase "It's not fair!" seemed to be one of the first combinations of words my own kids learned to say, right after "Daddy," "Mama," and "More!"

It's the essence of the first sibling story in the Bible. Adam and Eve, the first man and woman, had two sons, Cain and Abel. I don't know what kind of childhood Cain and Abel had growing up together, but it does seem that even in that fresh new world, without social media and designer labels and video gaming, one of the brothers picked up on the idea of fair and not fair.

As young men, Cain and Abel both made sacrifices to God. It just so happened that God preferred Abel's sacrifice over Cain's. Cain didn't like that one bit. He had his own version of stomping and door slamming. Scripture says,

> Cain lost his temper and went into a sulk. GOD spoke to Cain: "Why this tantrum? Why the sulking? If you do well, won't you be accepted? And if you don't do well, sin is lying in wait for you, ready to pounce; it's out to get you, you've got to master it." (Gen. 4:5–7 THE MESSAGE)

It seems to me that Cain didn't think God's response was fair.

God had good advice for Cain. God reminded him to shut down the tantrum and stay on alert, because Cain was opening up a door for sin by focusing on what he thought his brother had unfairly received. Cain didn't listen and went on to commit the first murder recorded in Scripture.

How quickly Cain moved from someone focused on what he

thought was right and fair to being someone who reacted in a truly unfair way by taking his brother's life.

I don't know what all the dynamics in Cain and Abel's relationship were. The Bible doesn't record details of their growing-up years. I don't know if perhaps Abel had always teased Cain or always seemed to get the best of everything while Cain struggled. Maybe Abel came off as the golden child, while Cain felt a bit ignored. Or maybe Cain was used to being the star, and Abel was something of a bratty little brother. Maybe Cain always tried to do the right thing, and it felt as if Abel always got away with murder. Until Cain did.

We won't know until we get to eternity what led up to Cain's reaction to God's response to his produce sacrifice and his brother's sacrifice from his flock. I don't really understand the difference between the sacrifices in God's eyes. But what I do know is that all too often, it is easy for me to slip into the kind of tantrum Cain experienced when something seems unfair.

This is the next place we journey through in the aftermath of a wrong happening to us: the Spiral of Fair. I can get caught here, playing out over and over the tangle of fair and unfair. I've spent a lot of time in this spin. Maybe you have too. It's dizzying and disorienting, and most importantly, it keeps us from moving forward. It's movement, but it's the kind that goes nowhere as we struggle to make our way toward healing and leaning on our Defender God.

To me, one of the toughest parts about being someone wired with a deep sense of fairness is that, in fact, there *are* things that are deeply unfair. There really are. There's the talented kid who worked all year in the drama department at school, staying after to work on sets and props and doing an incredible job in his audition. But the nephew of the drama teacher tried out for the same part and, you guessed it, won the role, even though he joked his way through the audition and forgot a bunch of his lines. There's the neighbor who whacks down those beautiful flowering shrubs you transplanted from your late grandmother's yard. He had the right to trim back what was growing over onto his property, but he certainly didn't need to massacre your landscaping in the process. There's the immigrant's experience of being brought to the United States at four months of age and then, years later, not being able to get into college because the DREAM Act has been revoked. And then there's the coworker who takes credit for your best ideas. She leaves your name completely out of the email she sent to your boss after the brainstorming meeting, and the next time you hear anything about your ideas, it's in an all-staff meeting where your coworker is giving a presentation that should have been yours and is getting all the kudos to boot.

Those situations truly aren't fair, and they often don't have neat, clean solutions. They can quickly become a never-ending round of he-said, she-said, each person giving a different version of the story—and there's no secret security tape showing what really happened, no wiretap on the phone to expose the true nature of the conversation, no private investigation that reveals all the facts.

To me, unfairness coming from friends and family seems more personal than hurts and wrongs that occur at the hands of strangers. If a stranger criticizes me rudely online, I don't like how I've been treated, but there's a degree of separation from the offender. I might not like it, but it doesn't feel personal. But if someone I know, someone I care about and esteem, makes a remark to the media about me or says something catty on my Instagram account, it's a whole different feeling. In both situations, a wrong has been committed. But it feels more unfair when it comes from someone in my day-to-day world. Because the wrong carries a different weight, I can be at even more risk of forgetting that sin is crouching at the door, waiting to see how I will conduct myself moving forward.

Is that true for you? Think about it: Is there a situation in your life that seems particularly painful because it involves a more personal connection? Do you find that it makes you consider the unfairness of the situation?

Here's one way you can know if you are focused on fairness: when you take your kids to get frozen yogurt, you do your best to make sure they all fill their yogurt cups to about the same level and only get one scoop of a topping. I mean, yes, we smart moms do this to avoid the whining should one of our kids get two ounces more than one of their siblings. But we also do it in the name of fair and unfair.

Here's another way you can tell: you count the presents under the Christmas tree and try to make sure there is the same number for each kid. Even when one of your kids is getting something pricier that takes almost all the amount you budgeted for each child, you feel compelled to make sure that that kid still has the same size gift stack, even if it means you have to wrap a pair of socks—separately—to make it all look "fair."

I feel you, sister. That's me too.

## AFTERMATH

In the days following the news that my sister, Jenni, had died in a plane crash, life was completely upside down. The intense emotion of disbelief carried me for a few days. Then the crashing collapse of a wave of reality hit my heart full force, a tsunami of grief that I thought would keep me tumbling and pushed down, unable to breathe beneath its greedy grasp. Then there would be days of numbness, a loss of all feeling, all the tears having scalded my soul to a scabbed and broken crust.

Through it all were details. Details that demanded attention. Details that had to be sorted. Details that required quick decisions and signatures, counsel and wisdom. Decisions about Jenni's funeral. Decisions about concert dates and events. Quickly it was revealed that I had been Jenni's choice to be her children's guardian and executor of her estate, and that brought a whole other level of details into my world. In some ways, managing all those details brought a sense of order to the chaos that had entered our lives. I moved from one stack of papers to another, from one conference call to another. Grief had to sift down through the cracks in the pile of tasks that had to be accomplished.

The weeks and months following Jenni's death were raw, endless, foggy, and hard. Even though it was so much more difficult and sad than I ever could have imagined, there was also a strange predictability to it. Of course it was going to hurt. Of course I would miss her so much sometimes that my lungs would feel like they couldn't draw air. Of course tears would start flowing at times of their own choosing, without my control. That's grief. That's expected.

What I didn't expect were the people who came out of the woodwork making claims about Jenni, about her work, her legacy, and her estate. You hear about that kind of thing, stories out of Victorian novels of the stranger who shows up at the death of a loved one, making some assertion of being owed this or that. But this was real life, not a story from a hundred years ago. It was unexpected, and wildly unfair.

I was determined to do right by my sister, and I wanted to

make sure I honored every wish and contract and dream she had left behind. Some requests showed up that I knew were what Jenni would have wanted. And some demands were not.

The most complicated situation I had to deal with was also pretty simple. A claim was made about a project that Jenni had been working on. We were moving forward with completing that project in Jenni's honor when an outside party showed up and claimed they were supposed to be involved at an extremely high level. I was surprised by this information, since I knew what my sister had told me about this particular project and her intentions for it. But I certainly wanted to have integrity in all of Jenni's uncompleted work. "Bring me the signed contract on this, and we'll figure it out," I said. Simple, right? Straightforward, correct?

No legitimate signed contract ever materialized. What did materialize was a very public lawsuit, full of unsubstantiated claims and unfounded assertions.

It rocked my sense of fair and unfair to the core. And what was simple—as in "no signed contract; no way"—turned into a very complicated legal situation.

I was scrambling to take on my sister's vast business and legacy in addition to becoming her children's guardian, doing my best to navigate and soothe their grief while managing my own. So many tasks and urgent responsibilities had to be completed following Jenni's passing, including complex business restructurings to fulfill her instructions that I be made the CEO of Jenni Rivera Enterprises. To have this lawsuit show up in the middle of everything—over something that had no paper trail, no contract, and nothing that substantiated the assertion—was overwhelming.

*Lord, why do I have to deal with this right now? It's so unfair!*

*Lord, how can this even be claimed? It's not what Jenni wanted. It's so unfair!*

*Lord, what is this going to do to my reputation? Here I am, an accidental CEO, and I want this organization to be able to lean on me. And now this? It's so unfair! And Lord, what will other people think of me? That's not fair at all!*

We had to call in the attorneys. They assured me that there was absolutely no valid legal or ethical claim in the situation.

"Then how come they can still take us to court? It's going to take so much time, not to mention the money!" I exclaimed.

While I'm educated enough in the law to know that people do this kind of thing all the time, taking baseless claims into the legal realm, it's a whole other situation when it happens to you.

The attorneys were great and thorough, and we prepared for our day in court to defend both my sister's legacy and her wishes. I was ready—ready to dig in for the long haul, ready to do whatever it would take to reverse the accusations and back talk that had occurred because of this situation. I would spend whatever time, resources, and passion were necessary to redeem my sister's memory and my good name.

It was on.

I told you before that I'm a fighter. I was mad and hurt enough to stay in the ring for what it took to win.

I was ready to ride in like a modern-day Joan of Arc. Joan was a simple girl who lived in the 1400s. When the English began attacking her home country of France, Joan had herself a journey. She had what she felt was a holy encounter with an angel telling her to fight on behalf of the French king against the invading English. With no prior experience as a soldier, and as a woman in a man's world, Joan rode against the enemy to defend her king, Charles VII. In the near term, it didn't look like much of a victory for Joan. She was captured by the English and went to trial. Ultimately, she was sentenced to death at the young age of nineteen. But twenty-five years after her death, the trial was reopened, and she was completely exonerated, found not guilty on the charges brought against her. The claims made against her were dropped, and five centuries later, she was proclaimed a saint by the Catholic church.[1]

Now, I was definitely hoping to skip the armed-combat portion of Joan's story, along with the burning-at-the-stake sentence she met. But I was definitely ready to ride into the thick of things as Rosie of LA, defender of my sister, and I was prepared for it to take a while.

The date for the courtroom fireworks to begin was getting closer and closer, and the attorneys had more and more meetings. One day the lead attorney gave me a call and asked me to come to his office because there had been some developments in the case he wanted to discuss. I left my office and met him in his team's conference room, everything gleaming chrome and glass. A carafe of ice water sat in the center of the broad conference table, condensation bubbling on the exterior of the crystal glasses surrounding it.

Noticing his expression, I took a big gulp of that silvery water, suddenly nervous about what he needed to tell me. He made some small talk, asking me about Abel and the kids, inquiring how my mom was doing. I replied with short answers, dreading to hear what he had called me there for but impatient to get it over with.

Clearing his throat, he began. "Well, I have an update. The other party wants to talk about a settlement—"

I shot out of my seat. "Absolutely not! Are you kidding me? We know this is a completely false claim! I want to see Jenni's name cleared! Why would we give in to this kind of thing?" I could barely catch my breath, I was so livid.

"Rosie," the attorney began gently, "arriving at a settlement does not mean we are agreeing with them or with their lawsuit. I want you to take a little time to think about what it would really mean to go through an entire court proceeding. The cost alone will be astronomical. By accepting the settlement agreement, you'll be able to resolve this situation at a much lower price tag and not have to spend more time on this thing. Now, part of the agreement would be that you couldn't discuss the details of the agreement. You'd have to let certain things go for the settlement to take effect, not the least of which is that you would have to let the other party off the hook, so to speak."

You better believe that I was not about a settlement. At all.

I was ready to spend whatever it took. I was ready to take whatever time it took. This wasn't fair! And I wasn't about to make it even more unfair by giving in.

That's what a settlement meant to me—that I was giving in.

I left the attorney's office with no intention of going with a settlement. But in that way he has, God began working on my heart. I started to feel his nudge that I needed to at least think about it. I was appalled at this nudge. I wrestled and prayed. I researched all the things. I kept spiraling back to the way this situation had made me feel, how it had been dragging my sister's memory through the mud, and how it was tarnishing my own reputation as well.

*God*, I prayed, *you know how unfair all of this is. There's no way you could want me to consider a settlement. Wouldn't it be . . . wrong?!*

I felt him impress these words on my heart: *Peace is worth more.*

That was profound, but it was not what I wanted to hear. I kept pressing in, kept begging and bargaining with God to make the other party not just drop the lawsuit but come crawling for an apology for everything they had put us through.

Through that pressing in, I started hearing these words land softly on my bruised heart: *Just trust me.*

I continued to restlessly wrestle with this idea in my mind and heart as the attorney left me message after message about needing to either decide for the settlement or write yet another huge check to keep the attorneys on retainer and get ready to do battle. Going to trial meant months and months of preparation, just as we were trying to learn a new normal as a family. But I was still caught in the dizzying spin of the unfairness of it all.

My conversations with God were filled with more proof of the ridiculousness of the situation, the baselessness of the other party's claims, the frustration of not seeing God's hand swoop in and make this right. He seemed quiet, but I needed his guidance.

One day it came. Quietly. Kindly. And sharp, all the same. *Let the ego die.*

I wanted to believe I had misheard. I wanted to believe that because I was in the right, he would never ask me to consider my own heart in the midst of this mess. Would he? How could that be fair? I wasn't the one who had started all this.

## UNFAIR TRIALS

As it turns out, I'm not the only follower of God to face an unfair trial. My Savior faced one, and much worse. The only person who has walked this earth without sin—Jesus—was accused of all kinds of things. His reputation was maligned, his motives were misunderstood, and it landed him in the highest court of

Jerusalem, in front of the governor of the region, Pilate. Matthew recorded what happened:

> When the leading priests and the elders made their accusations against him, Jesus remained silent. "Don't you hear all these charges they are bringing against you?" Pilate demanded. But Jesus made no response to any of the charges, much to the governor's surprise. (Matt. 27:12–14 NLT)

"But Jesus made no response to any of the charges." It still guts me, the image of Jesus allowing them to make all kinds of accusations about things that were not his intention or his heart. And they got away with it! The unfairness burns through me. And, I have to admit, this passage sometimes confuses me. After all, the same Jesus did this:

> When it was almost time for the Jewish Passover, Jesus went up to Jerusalem. In the temple courts he found people selling cattle, sheep and doves, and others sitting at tables exchanging money. So he made a whip out of cords, and drove all from the temple courts, both sheep and cattle; he scattered the coins of the money changers and overturned their tables. To those who sold doves he said, "Get these out of here! Stop turning my Father's house into a market!" His disciples remembered that it is written: "Zeal for your house will consume me." (John 2:13–17)

This is the same Jesus who told off the hyper-religious and those who lorded it over the people with their piety. This is the Jesus who minced no words in those situations. And let's not miss that John said he actually used a whip to drive people from the temple courts!

Can you imagine if that kind of situation occurred today? And yet the same Jesus who so valiantly and dramatically defended the poor and sick, who refused to allow people to be taken advantage of in the temple courts, and who didn't shy away from a debate also didn't speak up to defend himself in front of Pilate. Why?

Of course, as followers of Jesus, we tell ourselves it's because the accusations and the mockery of a court system and the cross had to happen for our salvation. But why specifically did Jesus not speak up for himself? The leading priests and elders still would have cried for his arrest and punishment, regardless of what he said. The path to the cross would have been the same. It wouldn't have changed things if he had piped up and made them aware of how unfair it was.

And then I find these words from Paul:

In your relationships with one another, have the same mindset as Christ Jesus:

Who, being in very nature God,
did not consider equality with God something to be used
to his own advantage;
rather, he made himself nothing
by taking the very nature of a servant,
being made in human likeness.
And being found in appearance as a man,
he humbled himself
by becoming obedient to death—
even death on a cross! (Phil. 2:5–8)

There it is: he humbled himself. Jesus didn't allow ego to become part of the picture. When he defended, it was for the cause of others. When he reprimanded, it was to uphold God's best. But when people made false claims against him, he was silent.

## EGO, LET GO

*Let the ego die.*

God's words kept working their way through my heart, gently sifting what was lurking there. He was right; well, of course he was. He's always right. As much as I didn't want to think so, there was some ego involved in this legal mess. I wanted to prove that I had been completely aboveboard and ethical in all my dealings on Jenni's behalf. A settlement would take that away from me. I thought I needed that public exoneration to soothe my heart.

And my ego.

Sigh.

God was right. When I let him prune back my ego, there were many important reasons to consider the settlement. It had been my sister's wish for me to oversee all that she left behind for us, and I was committed to being a good steward of that. To spend untold amounts of money to fight this lawsuit would not have been a good use of the resources Jenni had worked hard to earn. Somehow, in all the unfairness, my ego had risen up and grabbed the steering wheel, and as a result, I was no longer heading straight for setting things right but was veering dangerously into revenge and proving and "I'll show you."

I'm sure the attorney was surprised when I called back and asked to meet. I'm sure after my passionate refusals to consider the settlement, it seemed like whiplash when I told him it might be time to look at the details. After more prayer, lots of details to adjust, more prayer, and, yes, some very frustrated tears, I went forward with the settlement. No one was more surprised than I was.

Perhaps those on the other side of the issue were surprised too. I don't know. Perhaps they saw it as some kind of a partial victory, given the amount they were originally trying to sue for. Maybe some people out there interpret my fulfillment of the settlement as some kind of admission of guilt.

It isn't. Believe me, I stand just as staunchly today as I ever did by the conviction that my sister's projects have been completed in accordance with the law; with valid, signed contracts; and with her wishes. I can still get very worked up about the unfairness of what happened. There may be people out there, who, uninformed about how settlements work and what they mean, think that I "lost." Actually, I gained. I gained something powerful.

I gained time with my family when they needed me most, focusing on them and not on the marathon of stress a trial would have brought.

I gained a peace that is more valuable than a fight.

And I discovered that my ego can get all wrapped up in this spiral of fair and unfair.

What about you? What are you fighting for? If there were a way to settle today that thing that was done to you, that situation that has kept you in knots for weeks, months, or years, would you? Or would the fight—the burn to make sure you were heard right, understood right, seen right—keep adding fuel to a ravenous fire?

Out of a desire to see you set free, I want to ask you to pray an extremely dangerous prayer. See, the spiral of fair and unfair is not an easy one to escape. We enter its swirl thinking there is only one way out, at the bottom of the dizzying vortex, where we believe all will be revealed, and we'll be publicly absolved. But the spiral of fair and unfair doesn't always work that way.

Pray this:

*Lord God, search me and know me, just as your serv-ant David wrote in Psalm 139. Show me where this fight has veered from a fight for what is fair and where my ego has gotten involved. Show me what is a righteous way to settle this issue. Yes, Lord, I know it will cost me some ground, but I know the ground you have for me is blessed. Help me know how to stand as Jesus stood, silent before unfair accusers, his silence ultimately a loud proclamation of power and righteousness and love. Show me, Lord, and give me the courage to see it.*

*In the name of Jesus, amen.*

Sister, there is nothing wrong with having a strong sense of fair and unfair. I'm with you. But fair and unfair will always twist around each other in this broken world. Each exists in contrast to the other. Sometimes, to stay out of the spiral, you'll need to settle. To settle means that no one completely gets what they want, but it also means that you can exit the spin.

The word *settle* is actually an Old English word from the 1500s that meant a "long bench." And that's how I think of it. When we settle a fight, when we settle a court situation, when we settle, I see myself and the other person sort of agreeing to sit together on a long bench. We can keep our distance. We certainly don't have to agree on how it all went down or how it turned out. But we've stopped the spin. We are able to leave the Spiral of Fair. We've exited the twisting nausea. And we just sit with it, settled. It's not giving up. It's not changing your definition of what's right. But you can have back time. Focus. Emotion. Don't let what's unfair unfairly eat up more of your life and heart.

Fair and unfair, sitting on a long bench. That's its own kind of peace, the kind that parks ego off to the side and brings back a calm.

Then there's this: that same Jesus who was silent before his accusers said to his followers, "Settle matters quickly with your adversary who is taking you to court. Do it while you are still together on the way" (Matt. 5:25).

Listen to Jesus, both in what he says and in what he doesn't say, and find peace that surpasses fair and unfair. Sometimes the destination at the bottom of the Spiral of Fair is a long bench where an invitation awaits you, asking you to sit for a spell. I know it doesn't look like your preferred place of rest. But I promise you, sometimes it's where you need to go to catch your breath before you head out on the next part of the journey.

## BEFORE WE MOVE ON

1. Do you have a strong sense of fair and unfair? Where do you think that comes from?

2. When you have a disagreement with someone in your friend group, family, or community, does it seem even more unfair to you? Why or why not?

3. How hard is it for you to be willing to settle? Does it feel like giving up? What could you also be giving up by not coming to a settlement?

*four*

# THE ISLES OF IDOLATRY

## CIARA AND ME?

We're best friends. She just doesn't know it yet.

You know, Ciara? The incredible singer, songwriter, and model? The one with all those dance-worthy hits and the movie roles and the television appearances and the fashion? That Ciara.

That's my bestie, even if she hasn't gotten the memo about our friendship.

But one day she'll catch up to what I already know. We're destined to be soul sisters, BFFs, the whole deal. I love, love, love her music. And I think we can all agree that she's an even better dancer than J.Lo or Britney Spears.

You don't believe that? Fight me.

I tell everyone, all the time, that one day soon, Ciara and I are gonna become friends. I'm just going to keep confessing it.

Because of this deep future friendship I have with Ciara, you can imagine how ecstatic I was when I learned that she would be at the same Beautycon event I was scheduled to attend. Destiny, I tell you. Because of my work in the beauty industry, it's always an honor to be part of Beautycon. Beautycon is the ultimate experience of all things makeup, fashion, and personal wellness. The events are held once a year in Los Angeles, New York, and Tokyo, Japan. There are celebrities everywhere, from YouTube stars to business leaders. Makeovers for attendees are offered around every corner, as well as amazing concerts and inspirational talks. It's one of the highlights of my year, and I can't wait to see who they announce for the lineup. Beautycon has had Arianna Huffington and Kelly Rowland and Tina Knowles Lawson and Priyanka Chopra, just to shamelessly name-drop a few. Then there are all the freebies, all the makeup and skin-care samples! For any of us who love the beauty industry, it really is like Christmas in August. I've been honored to be a part of the team for the last several years. I'm proud to represent Latina women in the beauty industry.

And now, here was the news that Ciara was going to be performing at Beautycon. Well, then.

I brought my daughter with me and made my way through the crowd up to the very edge of the stage. I may or may not have thrown a few elbows to get up there. Listen, Ciara needs me in her life, and I'll do whatever it takes to get to her. The crowd around us was buzzing, waiting for her to come out. We were all there to support our girl.

The intro music started to build, and suddenly, there she was! Right in front of me, lyrics flying, dance moves on point. I was screaming and singing, jumping up and down. I knew every word, every dance move, and I was hitting every beat.

My daughter Kassey was horrified.

People around us started to recognize me and take pictures and video of my Ciara lyric-singing, dance-move performance. My daughter was mortified on two levels—one, that her mom was completely rocking out at a Ciara concert, and two, that people were videoing her mom doing so, and it would surely be all over social media by the end of the day.

I didn't care. I was having my best day ever.

Ciara is a believer, and her testimony about her life fires me up every time I hear it. I love how gently and yet unapologetically she has talked about her faith journey, how she and her husband, Russell Wilson, are living out their marriage under Christian precepts. Her lyrics are filled with references to forgiveness, redemption, and loving one another. I admire her as a woman, a business leader, a wife, a mom.

And a dancer, of course.

Between a couple of songs, Ciara took a moment to talk to the crowd, and she spoke about the difference between bitterness and beauty. There was so much power, so much wisdom in what she said, and when she paused to take a breath, I shouted out, "Preach it, girl!"

To be supportive, you know.

Ciara giggled, looked right at me, and said, "She said, 'Preach it, girl!'" and giggled again.

I told you guys. I told you. We're destined to be besties. This was a great first step.

Elated, I turned to look at my daughter next to me, wanting to make sure she had seen this confirmation of Ciara's connection to me. She was standing there, mouth wide open. "I've never seen you like this!" she hissed. "What is wrong with you?!"

What's wrong with me? Baby girl, it's all that's right! Ciara noticed me! Called me out! Interacted with me! One of these days, my daughter will understand the profound moment she got to witness.

The people who had already figured out who I was kept videoing. But for the people who didn't know me, Ciara acknowledging me extended her celebrity to me. I was now the girl in the crowd who told her to preach it! I've got to admit, I came out of that concert on cloud nine. I was a fangirl who had been seen by her dance idol, and it felt good.

I found out that Ciara was going to be on a panel the next day, and I couldn't wait for another opportunity to interact with her.

Now usually I'm someone who follows every rule to a tee. Tell me where the lines are, and I feel honor bound to stay within them. But, come on, this situation was an exception. I didn't technically have a ticket to the panel that Ciara was on. (And by technically, I mean I had no ticket. None. But whatever.) That technicality in this situation was not going to hold me back. I got to the room where her panel was being held and figured out a way to slip in. It was all going great until the security guard for the panel noticed me and wanted to see my ticket. I kept trying to tell him that I was also a Beautycon "talent" and begged him to let me stay. To no avail—he turned out to also be a rule follower to a tee and, ahem, escorted me out of the room. So, yeah, I managed to get kicked out of my own event.

Ciara, that's what friends do for each other. Future friends, that is.

Again, my daughter was aghast. She couldn't believe that her rule-following mama had engaged in such tactics *and* had gotten bounced out of a Beautycon event to boot. I keep kind of hoping she'll eventually give me a few points for being cool, but so far, no luck. Funny!

I had one more item on my Ciara list to achieve. Since we'd had that deep moment the day before—the one where she giggled and acknowledged that I had called out "Preach it!" in response to her awesome exhortation to the crowd—I figured I should reach out to her via social media, you know, just to stay in touch. I DMed her through Instagram and introduced myself.

"Hi, Ciara!" I wrote. "I'm Rosie Rivera and was at your amazing concert yesterday at Beautycon. I'm the woman who was on the front row, singing all the songs and doing all the dance moves. I'm also the one who told you to preach it when you were talking to the crowd. I just wanted to let you know how much I admire you and appreciate the work you do! And, as we all know, you're an even better dancer than J.Lo and Britney! Anyway, would love to connect! God bless!"

She hasn't DMed back yet.

It's fine.

It's fine.

## DANGEROUS ISLANDS

The ancient tale of the *Odyssey*, a classic that a lot of us had to read back in high school, is a Greek story about a man named Odysseus and his multiyear journey as he tried to make his way home after the Trojan War. Along the way, he encountered many challenges and strange sights. He had to overcome all kinds of obstacles. Many of his encounters took place on a series of islands. He visited the island of Lotus, a place where he was tempted to stop his journey and just live the easy life. He went to the island of the Cyclops, a horrible creature who tried to destroy Odysseus and his men. He almost went to the island of the Sirens, where disaster awaited, but he was able to plug his ears so he didn't hear the captivating call of the Sirens and thus avoided catastrophe. And on and on and on. Odysseus came into contact with so many islands, each with its share of possible resources to help Odysseus on his journey, or enemies who attempted to keep him from ever arriving home.

It's how I think of this next part of the journey you and I are on. There are some dangerous islands ahead, places I think of as the Isles of Idolatry. We must make it past them in order to fully rely on God as our Defender.

## IDOL THROWING

We throw around the word *idol* a lot in our culture. There's the show *American Idol*, the hit series in which people compete to become the next big music talent. When we admire someone for his profound preaching, we talk about "idolizing" him. After Jenni died, countless people told us or said in interviews that she had been their idol. We are pretty casual about the idea of someone being an idol, and we usually mean it in a flattering way about someone we admire.

Obviously, there are risks involved in idolizing any person. I've seen people idolize their spouses. I've seen people idolize a mentor or a teacher. I've seen people whose faith journeys were destroyed when the pastor they were following made poor personal choices. Those people had idolized that pastor, and when he proved he was just as susceptible to sin and temptation as the rest of us, it completely rocked their worlds. That's one of the ways you can identify whether you've elevated someone too high in your heart and mind: If that person were to disappoint you, would it be devastating or merely upsetting?

Looking back, I can see there have been plenty of times that I've idolized someone (Ciara doesn't count . . . ). Whenever we do this, it's not a great choice. It puts too much pressure and attention on the person our idolization is focused on. And most importantly, it dishonors God for us to put a human being above him in our affections, thoughts, and pursuits. It's dangerous because it sets us up for disappointment, and it takes our eyes off God.

There is another kind of idolization we need to be equally, if not even more, vigilant about avoiding: the idolization of revenge. It's the first Isle of Idolatry we need to navigate in our journey for justice.

That's right. It's very possible to make an idol out of the wrong you have suffered, out of the situation or person who hurt you. That might sound a little confusing if you associate an idol only with a celebrity or someone you admire. But an idol is anything, *anything*, that becomes much bigger in our lives than our God. And I believe that the times when we've been wronged, when we want to see someone pay for what they did to us, well, those can become the biggest focus in our world.

Revenge can become our unwanted, resented, thorny idol that we revisit and speak about over and over.

Think about it. That lady who kept honking at you yesterday in the school pickup line, the one who was convinced that you should pull out into oncoming traffic just because she seemed to think that her manicure appointment was more important than you getting your babies home safely—how long did you continue to think about her? Did a fantasy arise after you got home, one in which you exited your car and told her what for? Did you call a friend and tell her about this impatient woman and her rude honking? How much of the rest of your afternoon and evening were taken up with brooding about her and her behavior and what you wish you had done in retribution?

There you go. A little idol. Not one of epic proportions—not just yet. But the building blocks are all there, and the next time you encounter her, if she's rude again or doesn't apologize, even more thought will go into building an internal revenge scheme. Oh, you may never actually confront her. But the altar is there all the same—a place in your mind where you go to revisit her rudeness and behavior.

The bigger the hurts in our lives, the bigger the idols. The abuser, the toxic parent, the friend who stabbed you in the back.

These idols in your life can become so big they squeeze out all thoughts of happiness and fulfillment.

You might be thinking, *Whoa, Rosie! Yes, I think a lot about what happened to me. And yes, I have strong emotions about that. But I don't think I'd elevate it to idol status!*

Sweet sister, please hear me. I've been there. Heavens, I'm still there in a couple of situations in my life. I don't have it all figured out. But what I do know is that when I allow the understandable bitterness and resentment toward someone who has wronged me to be front and center in my thoughts, I veer into idolatry.

The apostle Paul warned against this. In his letter to the church at Colossae, he shared a lot of wisdom about being on guard for these kinds of feelings. In Colossians 3:5 he wrote, "Mortify therefore your members which are upon the earth; fornication, uncleanness, inordinate affection, evil concupiscence, and covetousness, which is idolatry" (KJV). I know in this translation, some of Paul's writings can sound like lines from a Shakespeare play, but let's break it down together. Take a look at that phrase *inordinate affection*. I did a little deep dive into what that phrase is in the original Greek language of the Bible, and here's what I found. It's the word *pathos*, which is defined as follows:

1. whatever befalls one, whether it be sad or joyous
   a. [specifically] a calamity, mishap, evil, affliction
2. a feeling which the mind suffers
   a. an affliction of the mind, emotion, passion
   b. passionate deed
   c. used by the Greeks in either a good or bad sense[1]

Did you catch that? "Inordinate affection" can actually refer to having too strong a connection to something that has happened to us, especially if that thing is a calamity or an evil. And it's part of a list that Paul called idolatry.

We are at risk of making a couple of things idols when we have been hurt. One is the deep desire to see people pay for what they did. We can obsess over it, put it as the primary thing we see on the windshields of our lives. While we're stuck in traffic, we compose and practice over and over the telling-off speech we're going to give that boss for the horrible way he treated us.

But here's the other part of the equation, the place I have gotten stuck more times than I'd like to admit. It's another Isle of Idolatry where we can get stranded on the shore.

It is the desire for people to acknowledge and understand what they did to us and how it made us feel. We think we might be able to move on if we know for certain that the other person is sorry and has fully experienced the depth of our hurt. But rarely do we get that satisfaction. We can press and push the other person to completely feel what we experienced, but often they won't.

When we don't get that resolution, we can obsess over how to get it. We can come to believe that the only thing that will allow us to heal is to see the other party experience a worthy revenge. When that obsession takes hold, we begin to worship an idol of revenge, trusting it as the only thing that can repair our broken hearts.

I wanted so badly for the man who sexually abused me not just to own up to what he did but also to show me that he felt bad about it. That he would take it back if he could. That he understood how his actions cost me, robbed me of my childhood, set a course for my early life that sent me spiraling into self-destruction. I thought that if and when that happened, I would be healed. I allowed his future possible repentance and acknowledgment to become this powerful potential balm, the needed medicine for my battered heart.

It didn't happen. And I teetered at the edge of idolatry.

At times I've felt very righteous about my feelings toward the things that have happened to me and the instigators. I'm one of those people who can be ready to tangle, ready to rush in and make things right and fire the cannons. I hate it when bad people seem to get away with bad things. For some reason, I've often thought that if I could just focus enough on what happened and who did it, then it would somehow keep it at the top of the list in God's mind too. That has felt like a good thing to me, something proactive in situations where I have felt less than empowered. But in doing that, I've overstayed my welcome on one of the Isles of Idolatry. I've spent so much time there that I've set up shop and started painting the walls. But I was never meant to live there. I'm called to journey on to wholeness.

I stand convicted. How about you?

## ANOTHER ONE OF THE ISLES

I find it interesting that Paul wrote strongly about idolatry to the church at Colossae. For some reason, I've always thought of idol worship as more of an Old Testament problem and believed that idolatry isn't mentioned all that much in the New Testament. But here's something interesting about Colossae: it was known for having a lot of people who were involved in an angel cult.[2] They worshiped the archangel Michael, perhaps because he is often referred to as the archangel who protects and who leads the army of God against evil.[3] That sounds like a great thing, to honor someone who keeps terrible people away from you and punishes those who come against you. But Paul was very clear to the church at Colossae that this was a foolish thing to do. He wrote, "Let no one defraud you of your prize [your freedom in Christ and your salvation] by insisting on mock humility and the worship of angels" (Col. 2:18 AMP). It costs us our ultimate freedom and peace in Christ when, instead of relying on God, we start relying on our own rage or on someone we think could gain our vengeance for us.

In their mythology, the ancient Greeks had a goddess called Adrestia, which means "she who cannot be escaped." She was the goddess of revenge and was said to have been the daughter of the god of war, Ares. She was also known by the name Nemesis, a word we still use today to describe an ultimate enemy. There were those who worshiped her and sacrificed to her for the revenge they thought she could bring down on their enemies.[4]

That's the risk of another one of the Isles of Idolatry: making others our saviors who will rescue us from the hurt we have experienced, who will right the wrong, who will charge in and fix it all. We idolize them, their ability, and their fighting spirit above the God who gave them those abilities.

## SAILING UP THAT MOUNTAIN

I went on a journey after Jenni died in a plane crash in 2012—an actual journey. About three months after the accident, I went with my mom and my three brothers, Juan, Pete, and Gus, to hike to the crash site. We flew from the United States to Mexico and then drove for hours and hours out into a remote region of Mexico. The roads went from poorly paved streets to scraped-dirt lanes to rough tracks etched into the earth. We drove as far as we could out into the wilderness, and then it was time to lace up our hiking boots and hike the rest of the way in.

Jenni's plane went down on December 9, 2012. The crash site was on a mountaintop south of Monterrey, Mexico, near Iturbide, which is just across the border from Texas. The area was named for a general from the early 1800s, Agustín de Iturbide, whose military success during the Mexican War of Independence ultimately led to him becoming emperor of Mexico in 1822.[5] Jenni had performed the night before in Monterrey and headed out the following morning to fly to her next date. But just sixty miles into the flight, over Iturbide, something went terribly wrong. The plane had reached a cruising altitude of twenty-eight thousand feet when it lost contact with air traffic control and went into a tailspin. Investigators told us it went down fast, and they didn't know why or exactly what had happened.

In the days following the crash, we had to rely completely on the accounts of the investigators who went to the site and recovered the remains and plane parts. It wasn't that we didn't trust them, but as a family, we kept having this nagging sense of "What if she survived and is there somewhere on the mountain?" There was so much that was unanswered about the crash. Over time, it became apparent that my brothers and my mom and I needed to go to the site. We needed to see the place for ourselves. We needed to be in the place Jenni was when she went home to God. We needed to know that she wasn't still there, waiting for us to come find her.

I know that could all sound a little strange to you. But I'm telling you, it wouldn't let go of me, this urgency that we needed to get there.

Jenni was the first to know something about me, something we later told family and friends but that I entrusted to her first: I was pregnant. Abel and I had been trying for a while, and Jenni had been my confidante and encourager as the months passed and the pregnancy tests still came up negative. When I learned I was finally pregnant in the fall of 2012, Jenni was the first to know. As the weeks passed following Jenni's death and my belly started to show, it was a strange mix of heavy grief and unsettled joy. I needed my sister to get through all this, but my sister was gone.

In March 2013, three months after Jenni died, my mom and brothers and I made the trek. My mom was sixty-five years old, and I was five months pregnant. We didn't really know what we were in for physically or mentally.

The gentleman who owned the land where the crash site was located was our guide. He was incredibly kind to us. He told us he wanted to give us the land where the crash had occurred, a generous gesture we declined, but we so appreciated his willingness to allow the land to be in our keeping and control if that would ease our hearts. We bounced along in our vehicles down those rough ruts until we couldn't take the cars any farther; then we set out on foot.

Iturbide is nine thousand feet above sea level, the same altitude as several ski towns in Colorado, like Telluride and Silverton. Your body feels that elevation change immediately; your lungs have to work harder to get enough air, and it makes everything tougher, whether you're just taking in scenery or hiking a rigorous trail. For someone my mom's age, and for me in my pregnant state, the altitude made for even more of a challenge.

Reaching the crash site required a five-hour hike over extremely tough terrain. This hike was not the kind you take at a beautiful national park, complete with well-marked trails and direction and mileage signs along the way. This was completely untamed wilderness on private property, involving terrain few humans ever had access to. As we set out on foot, with the landowner leading the way, it felt as if we had arrived at the edge of the earth, no sights or sounds of human civilization for our eyes or ears to behold. We heard only a lonely wind and the occasional call of a solitary hawk. The local guide marked the way.

The first few steps of the hike were emotional; it made the catastrophe more immediate, more real. The landowner was in the lead; one of my brothers was behind him, then me, then another brother, then my mom, and then my other brother behind her. We would climb, silently, breathing heavily, the crunch of our hiking boots punctuating the quiet. By some unspoken agreement, we would stop for a bit. We'd drink water, squint at the sun, and ask a few quiet questions of the landowner about the animals found in the area and some of the foliage. Then we would begin again, the mountainside growing more and more steep.

I don't know how my mom made the climb. I don't know how I did. But we wouldn't quit. We couldn't quit. Jenni needed us. And we needed her.

As we continued to ascend, I put in my earbuds and listened to my favorite praise and worship music. I focused on God, on the words, on feeling his presence. We each found long walking sticks that helped us with the steep climb, and we pushed our sticks into the dirt, pulling our way up the rocky ground. We climbed and climbed as the sun climbed even higher, and I lost all sense of time—just one step, then the next, then the next.

Then we were almost there.

We knew we were almost there because we began to see airplane parts. Peppered across the ground, the shredded metal and blackened bits stood out as clearly wrong and so out of place in this rugged wilderness. Even though we knew this was what we had climbed for, it was still a shock when this broken evidence of a man-made presence came into view. We hiked a few more yards, and that's when we saw a pair of jeans. A woman's makeup bag. A shoe. The contents of the passengers' luggage, caught in the branches of the scrub pines, rippling in the breeze.

It reminded me anew. Yes, our greatest grief was for Jenni. But there were seven people who lost their lives that day in December. The two pilots. Jenni's makeup artist. The hairdresser. Her publicist. Her attorney. And Jenni. To see these artifacts from their lives, the remnants of possessions they had carried with them that day, was shocking. It brought the tragedy dramatically home in the most ordinary way, through the leftover laundry of their lives. It was a banner declaring "Death Happened Here." We didn't touch anything on the mountainside. We wanted to respect the site; we wanted to honor all seven of them.

A cross had been placed by the landowner and those who had come to investigate the accident. The site was still blackened where the largest portion of the plane had met the earth. I took it all in and waited for the emotional wave to hit me, to knock me down in its violence. I had tried to prepare myself ahead of time, ready for another wave of anguish and loss to drown me on this dry mountainside.

But of the emotions I expected to feel, nothing prepared me for what showed up.

Peace. A sense of beauty. Love. Grace.

It was unlike anything I had expected.

As I stood there, knowing that was the place where my sister had gone home to God, I had the answer for why I had needed to come. *I rescued her*, I thought. *This was a rescue mission*. It was a rescue mission in that I felt I had come for my sister; I had shown up for her. I had endured the difficulty of the journey to get there.

It had finally been my turn to rescue her.

Throughout our lives together, Jenni had usually been the one coming to my rescue. She had been my defender in many situations. I relied on her as my big sister to come to my aid, to step in between me and those who threatened me. Jenni was my world in many ways. Of course, we had the occasional sisterly spat. She wasn't perfect, and neither am I. But those moments would send me completely sideways and wreck me, far out of proportion to whatever the issue was. Twisted in with missing her after she died was something inconsolable, something so much heavier than I could bear.

That day on the mountain and in the days following, I began to understand. God was gentle in the way he showed me, but when he showed me, it was clear. He spoke to my heart. *You had made your sister an idol, Rosie. You'd given her so much more time and focus than you did anything else in your life. Anything you thought was a slight or a disagreement with her, you always took to such a deep personal level. You depended on her to be your defender, your advocate, and your counsel. You had made your sister an idol. The peace you feel is because you will now be able to love her freely again as your sister, as a human.*

*Yes, Lord*, I thought. *That is exactly it.*

I had done that. Jenni as my big sister, Jenni as the fearless performer and business woman, Jenni as the passionate woman, Jenni as the devoted mom—I had thought of her as the person who could fight and win my battles, who could set things right for me, who would be the first person I could run to in any situation. I would say out of affection that Jenni was my idol.

But it turned out she really was.

That's another Isle of Idolatry we can become shipwrecked on: that place where we pin all our hopes on another person to make a situation right. Perhaps it's your husband, whom you expect to go make it right with the neighbor who is violating your fence line. Perhaps it's the HR manager at work you are leaning on to deal with the unfair boss. Perhaps it's the attorney you've hired to get that back child support. God's great and all, but you are really leaning on this person or this organization or this news agency to set things right, to clear your reputation, to expose the wrong. If my husband were just the right kind of guy . . . If my HR manager were competent . . . If I could just afford that high-powered attorney, then everything would turn out right!

That's—wait for it—idolatry, putting a human being's abilities above God's.

Does it mean you shouldn't have help when it comes to dealing with injustices that have been committed against you? No. If your husband is great at stepping in, awesome. If your HR manager knows how to kick butts and take names, fantastic. If that high-powered attorney is available, spectacular. But keep your security and your hope in God, and let those talented individuals in your life remain human.

I want to encourage you to embrace and hold tight to the truth I realized up on that mountain that day. You have people you need to release from the role of being your defender. You need to let them be humans in your life, not saviors. There is only one Savior: Jesus Christ our Lord. Not your pastor. Not your mentor. Not your spouse. Not your parent. Don't allow yourself to run aground in this journey toward God as your Defender. Anytime you put your hope in a human over the Holy One, you have come ashore on another Isle of Idolatry. And this place was never meant to be your home.

We left that mountainside site where Jenni left this earth and made our way back down the craggy terrain, back to the cars, back down the pockmarked road. When I looked back at that mountain, God had left a verse crafted in his Word for me:

> I lift up my eyes to the hills.
>> From where does my help come?
> My help comes from the LORD,
>> who made heaven and earth. (Ps. 121:1–2 ESV)

I don't know which Isle of Idolatry you might be stuck on. Maybe it's the one where you've made an idol out of what happened to you. Maybe it's the one where you are waiting for an acknowledgment and apology from the person who hurt you. Maybe, like me, you're stuck with thinking another person will be your defender. But I'm asking you today to leave that idol behind. Get God back in your windshield. Head toward him at full speed and plug your ears to the call of distraction. He is your hope and your rescue.

## BEFORE WE MOVE ON

1. Which Isle of Idolatry do you think you might be stuck on?
2. How did you get there?
3. What makes you nervous about leaving that place? Is it the fear that people will get away with what they did to you? Is it that you have so much trust in the person who is pursuing justice for you?

*five*

# THE QUICKSAND OF
# SELF-DESTRUCTION

WHEN I WAS A KID, FLIPPING THROUGH CHANNELS late on a Saturday afternoon as if it was my job (and when you're a kid with no bills to pay, who's also bored, TV surfing *is* your job), I'd sometimes stumble across a station showing old movie classics. Many times I'd zoom on by, finding the stilted dialogue and grainy black-and-white images not all that exciting. But every so often, a scene would keep me chained to the television, and not because it was something I really wanted to see. Usually it was something I would watch from between my fingers, my hands clasped over my face, eyes partially covered but also peering out, not wanting to watch but watching.

What I would be watching was often an old scary movie.

It would typically involve some rogue dinosaur churning its way through a major metropolitan area. Or it might be a generic Dracula character who really should have come off as pretty comical in an overly dramatic, grainy-film way (but who always managed to freak me out anyway). Every now and then, there would be a scene that seemed scarier to me than giant reptile city smashers or undead Romeo stereotypes. A scene that was a classic and yet was still terrifying. A situation that had no monsters or mummies but was just as sinister and foreboding.

I speak, of course, of the quicksand scenario.

You know what I'm talking about. A young, beautiful couple is trying to flee from danger. They make their way into the jungle, hands clasped, young love propelling them to run faster. And then it happens. The boyfriend takes one more stride and begins to sink, the path turning into a deadly soup of sand and hidden water, sucking the beloved into its mysterious depths, the girl-friend still on stable ground desperately trying to pull her guy back to safety.

All to no avail.

The quicksand bubbles one more time, the guy's handsome face disappears, and only the deceptive surface of the quicksand is left, all evidence of its carnivorous activity gone. The girlfriend shrieks her beloved's name one more time and then hears the crackling of a branch in the distance. She jumps to her feet, gives one more longing look at the quicksand, and then scurries, sob-bing, farther into the jungle.

Or some such scene like that.

The characters would be different from time to time; their reasons for being out where secret quicksand pits lurk would vary. Sometimes it was the good guy who got sucked down in the goo. Sometimes it was the bad guy in a much more satisfying turn of events. Regardless, I found it terrifying and mesmerizing that you could be making your way on an average hike, and the path beneath your feet could turn to thick liquid and slurp you down to the center of the earth, never to be seen again.

It wasn't long into my childhood that I first stumbled into my own quicksand of sorts. It would be a long, long time before I figured out how to get out.

## REVENGE, THE ROLLING STONE

The quest for revenge, for vindication, is a dangerous one. "Revenge . . . is like a rolling stone," wrote clergyman Jeremy Taylor back in the 1600s in his sermon "Apples of Sodom," "which, when a man hath forced up a hill, will return upon him with a greater violence, and break those bones whose sinews gave it motion."[1]

What the good pastor Taylor is telling us here is that revenge is something we can push for and work for, but it can turn on us, breaking us in ways we never expected. The pursuit of revenge, in our timing, in our own wisdom, can become a self-destructive force in our lives, a quicksand that takes us down.

When God acts as our Defender, it ultimately leads to good for us. When we act as our own defenders, doing it our own way, it can lead to even deeper hurt and destruction in our lives. We see it play out in the stories of others around us. Your best friend has had it up to here with her critical mother-in-law, and they finally have that knock-down, drag-out fight that's been brewing. But now your friend's marriage is punctured because of her husband's impossible position of trying to honor his mom and love his wife well. Self-destruction.

You see it on the job, where you try to get back at the co-worker who's been taking credit for your work. You vent about the situation to someone you consider a friend at work, but then that person rats you out, and you find yourself hauled into an HR meeting. Self-destruction.

Or you're tangling with the spouse who left you, fighting through your attorneys over custody issues and money, and the environment is getting more and more heated. You understandably want him to pay for what he's done, for his unfaithfulness. But your kids are getting dragged through the muddy pit of all the emotions involved. Self-destruction.

In my own life, more times than I'd like to count, I've rolled a rock of revenge up a hill, only to have it backfire on me and topple me down.

# THE WEIGHT OF HURT

It wasn't as if I set out to gain fifty pounds the year I turned twelve years old, but that's what happened.

After experiencing sexual abuse beginning at the age of eight, I was filled with resentment and hate. I didn't have anyone to talk to about what had happened to me—no counselor, no trusted mentor. I stuffed resentment down into the core of myself, storing it up, and that resentment and fury and anger began to grow. Over the next few years, from the age of eight until I was twelve, a constant secret fury was my inner song.

The year I turned twelve, I was walking through a restaurant when an older male, an adult, whistled at me. He kept trying to get my attention, making remarks and gestures about my figure. I was terrified—and livid. I started wearing really baggy clothes and supertight bras to squash my growing cleavage, all in an effort to hide and protect myself. And I started to eat.

The person who had abused me was still someone I had to deal with on a regular basis in my life. One day, when I was a preteen, he came by the house to pick up his kids and told me that I looked terrible in my baggy clothes getup. He warned me that if I kept gaining weight, it would make me ugly and fat. He looked at me with utter disgust instead of his usual inappropriate leering.

Something clicked deep inside me. This, *this* was the answer I had been looking for. If I started gaining weight, then I could keep people like him away from me. Eating also seemed to fill a void in me, to quiet some of the rage. I could exact some revenge on my abuser by turning into someone who seemed to disgust him.

So I started eating more. And more. And more.

But that stone started rolling back on me. I was now eating addictively, unable to stop myself. The pounds kept piling on.

Within a year, I weighed more than two hundred pounds, which, on my smaller frame, was wildly unhealthy for me.

It worked to keep my abuser away. But now I had a new problem.

I liked boys. I wanted their attention. But I didn't. But I did. And that extra weight was now creating a different kind of self-sabotage. I already felt unworthy and dirty because of the abuse I had suffered. Now I despised the way I looked and my lack of control when it came to eating. Even more important, I was compromising my health by being at a weight that put me at risk for a variety of health issues. The wheels really came off when I discovered that my abuser had also abused my niece. I blamed myself, believing that because I hadn't disclosed what he had done to me, I had set her up for the same wrong to happen to her.

Then I started to push the revenge rock in another direction. I decided to dramatically lose weight.

For a whole year, from the age of thirteen until I turned fourteen, I only ate a little bit of cereal a day. I worked out constantly, wrapping myself in plastic bags to make myself sweat even more. I drove my mom crazy when I would work out upstairs to an aerobics tape, my footsteps pounding to the beat of the music thumping from my bedroom, echoing into the downstairs living area.

That extreme weight-loss approach brought on a different kind of pain, all still driven by the desire for vindication. With the weight gain, I was trying to get back at my abuser, to make him question why he had ever targeted me. With the weight loss, I trying to get back at him again, to prove that a good guy, that guys in general, would want what he had tried to ruin.

But I was hurting myself physically, emotionally, and spiritually.

By the age of fifteen, I had lost quite a bit of weight and was looking better. Then I was assaulted again. There was a boy who had started to notice me. I went out on a date with him but had no intention of having sex with him. During the date, he let me know that he had a gun in the trunk of the car. He pulled up to a hotel, claiming that a friend of his had forgotten something in one of the hotel rooms, and he had volunteered to pick it up for him. With the knowledge that he had a weapon, I followed him up to the hotel room on his "errand," and once we were in the room, he overpowered me. He wasn't violent per se, but I was scared and overwhelmed. As crazy as this sounds now, after that night, he considered me his girlfriend and pursued me, driving by my house at all hours, serenading me. At that point, I thought, *What does it matter? At least he wants me.*

When I look back on my thought process, it seems incredibly sad. I thought my body wasn't worth anything. A pedophile had stolen my virginity when I was eight years old. Virginity had been placed at such a high value that once it was gone, I thought it was the treasure, not me.

What ensued were years of getting involved with bad guys who would take me out only to have sex with me. I covered the pain by drinking, a habit that started when I was just thirteen. As the years went by and the number of guys I was with increased, so did my risky behavior. I moved from drinking to heavy drinking. I went from having sex with a guy who thought he was my boyfriend to meeting up with random guys to have casual sex. I knew I was at risk for any number of sexually transmitted diseases. I knew the drinking was destructive. I hated what I was doing. Yet I seemed powerless to stop it.

My attempts to get back at my original abuser had led me

down a dangerous path in a terrifying jungle, and the quicksand of self-destructive behavior seemed ready to swallow me up.

## A DANGEROUS SELF

In the Bible, Nabal was a guy set on vengeance. We read about him in 1 Samuel 25. He was a wealthy man with lots of livestock, and he was married to a wise and beautiful woman named Abigail. One day, a guy named David entered the region. David would ultimately become the king of Israel, but at this point, he had put together something of a personal security business. He and his buddies would guard livestock flocks from people roaming the countryside looking to steal sheep and goats. I guess in his own way, he was something of a guardian cowboy, giving out his own version of Old West justice. David and his pals spent some time protecting Nabal's flocks and then had a servant approach Nabal, asking for payment for the service they had provided.

Nabal was furious. He hadn't asked for this kind of protection and wasn't about to put any money or resources on the table for David and his men. He sent the servant back to David with words of anger and insult. David was livid in return. Eager to participate in some rigorous bloodletting, he had his men get their swords ready and made plans to go violently confront Nabal.

A servant, realizing how quickly the situation was escalating, went to Nabal's wife, Abigail, and explained the situation. Abigail had a cool head on her shoulders, and she came up with a plan. She got some good food and gifts together, climbed onto her Bible-times SUV (also known as a donkey), and headed out to meet with David. With grace and wisdom, she negotiated peace with David, defusing the issue on his side. Crisis averted, she made her way home with what should have been good news.

That's not how Nabal saw it. When she let Nabal know that no violence would be necessary to settle the issue, he was so furious at missing his chance for revenge that he had what Bible scholars think was a stroke. He died a few days later. His inability to accept a peaceful outcome to his dispute with David ultimately cost him his life. Self-destruction.

I'm not saying that if you have been the victim of a terrible situation, you are just like the hotheaded Nabal. But what I am saying is that when we believe we have been wronged, we are all in danger of taking on behaviors and actions that are ultimately the most dangerous to us.

The funny thing is, when I read the story of Nabal, I kind of get his point. He hadn't asked for David's help and justifiably didn't think he owed him anything. I think about what would happen if people showed up and decided to cut my grass for me when I hadn't asked them to and then rang the doorbell and held out their hands for payment. Yes, they did the job, but it was a job I didn't hire them for. I'd probably be pretty ticked too. As Nabal said,

> "Who is this David? Who is this son of Jesse? Many servants are breaking away from their masters these days. Why should I take my bread and water, and the meat I have slaughtered for my shearers, and give it to men coming from who knows where?" (1 Sam. 25:10–11)

But Nabal couldn't accept the peaceful solution Abigail had put together. He was mad, and he wanted heads to roll. When he didn't get that, his own internal state literally cost him his life.

My own internal state has come close to costing me my life too. But for some reason, I thought it was a way to make my abuser pay.

I'm pretty sure it never affected him, but it surely affected me.

## QUICKSAND BABY STEPS

God's mercy is incredible to me. After all, I'm a living example of it, and you are too. We've faced terrible things. We've been deeply hurt. We are still seeking and walking and learning and growing. His mercy is sufficient to cover and heal the things we've done in an effort to get back at those who have hurt us.

Part of the way we experience God's mercy is to do something that is hard for us: receive it. That seems like such a vague thing, doesn't it? Just receive it. What does that actually look like?

For me, after all the terrible relationships with guys who were only after sex, after the drinking, after sinking in a self-destructive quicksand, I finally began making my way back to God. I slowly began digging back into his Word. With baby steps, I started to pray with more consistency and faith. Eventually, the destructive sexual behaviors slowed down. I was able to work with a great counselor. I got deeply involved in a solid church family. I stopped the drinking. It was a process, it was hard, and it took me a long time to come to a deeper understanding of why I had acted out the way I had when my actions were repugnant to me.

It doesn't mean that I completely did away with self-destructive behaviors.

Now, as an adult, I still catch myself pushing people away. Whenever I am going through a problem, I tend to isolate myself.

It's how I try to lower the risk of someone rejecting me, of someone seeing the "real me" and deciding I'm not worthy enough. Those echoes from my childhood abuse still haunt me, just in a new form.

I'll find myself behaving in ways that I can rationally look at and know don't make sense. I will sometimes purposely not leave a good first impression; that way, no one will be surprised later by the "real" Rosie. I know I could tell you everything you want to hear. I know I could get myself all painted and prettied up and present myself as thoroughly sweet and light. But I would rather you meet the raw Rosie than be disappointed later. And if you can't handle the raw Rosie, well then, at least I haven't risked more time and investment in the relationship only to get hurt later.

Yep. These are the borders of the quicksand of destructive behavior. Some of it is good and protective, and some of it is still a reaction rather than a powerful approach.

I've made it hard on my friends at times. My best friends have seen me through it all, have experienced me pulling away and bracing myself for rejection, and they've still hung on. I thank them so much for the way they won't let me get away with letting go.

Here's the good news for you and me. We can get better. We can identify the ways that our hurts and our pursuits of revenge have cost us in the past, and we can challenge ourselves to press on.

Recently I had a business meeting in Monterrey with a social media influencer about an opportunity that could benefit us both. In the days leading up to the meeting, I was all in my head. I had already decided that she wasn't going to like me, that I could just be standoffish and save myself from the rejection that would ultimately come.

But then I recognized what I was doing. I was still operating from a place of allowing my abuser to control my today. By God's grace, I decided to go into that meeting from a different perspective. I went in as a daughter of God, a daughter God advocates for and loves. I went in not as someone running from ghosts but as someone running toward a future God holds for her. I told myself, *Rosie, you're going to change. You're not going to go in scared.*

And guess what? The influencer and I hit it off. We loved each other. We had a great series of meetings, and I look forward to what our collaboration might hold. I like to think that even if she hadn't liked me, even if it felt like some of my old tapes started playing in my head, by going in not trying to prove my worth or hedge my bets, I still would have walked out of those meetings a better person.

Sister, it is possible. If this girl who was going pro in quicksand-sinking can do it, I know you can too.

God's Word says, "My grace is sufficient for you, for my power is made perfect in weakness" (2 Cor. 12:9). *Sufficient* means that his grace is enough—enough to carry us, enough to let us live better—even when the abuser is still out there, even when the mean boss went on to get a promotion, even when the former friend has moved on to a new group. It doesn't say that revenge is sufficient; it says his grace is. Revenge can never satisfy and heal. It can help make a wrong right. It can potentially help us close a chapter. But only grace can restore us and bring us to wholeness.

## THE COST OF QUICKSAND

Obviously, the girl-gone-wild days of my teenage years in response to cataclysmic hurts and wrongs in my childhood cost me deeply.

But it was several years before I identified other ways in which I was allowing an unresolved injustice to bleed me. I share these next concepts because these might be areas that are costing you, too, and you may not have realized it.

Because my deepest wound from childhood was caused by a man, I assumed that almost all men were bad. Now, looking back, I can see how profoundly sad that was. There were good men in my life, men who loved well and were protective and knew how to honor women. But in an effort to protect myself, I had unconsciously lumped all guys into one category and one mythology. "All guys are after one thing: sex." I would tell myself this over and over. "Men get what they want, and then they leave" was another mantra of mine. I saw a possible child abuser in every guy. In holding this view, I was justifying my bitterness and toxicity. I missed some lovely guys along the way, men I could have had friendships with, men I could have learned from, men who could have cared for me.

Now let me be very clear here. I am not blaming victims for what has happened to them. If your husband, in the midst of what you thought was a vibrant and healthy marriage, up and left you out of the blue for a coworker, I am not telling you that you are at fault. If you have a childhood-abuse story similar to mine, I am absolutely not saying that you somehow bear responsibility in the matter. If you experienced being bullied at the bus stop as a kid, I'm not saying you brought it on yourself. By whatever means and in whatever timing you have experienced hurt, I'm not putting it on you.

But what I am saying is that I gathered up bitterness and toxicity and held it to my heart as my own version of armor. I clung tightly to that bitterness and toxicity, even though I knew God was calling me to lay it down. It was a security, it was an old friend, and it was the thing I used to continue to engage in self-destructive behaviors.

For years it cost me almost every rich, beautiful, and in-depth relationship I could have had, relationships that God could have used to heal me more quickly.

When I was twenty-one, with multiple unhealthy relationships with men swirling around me, my precious dad sat me down on the couch to talk with me. "Daughter," he asked, tears in his voice, "why don't you love me?" It was easier to push him away than to work through the complexity of how another male figure in my life had assaulted me. It seemed easier to keep all men at bay, including my loving father.

That bitterness and toxicity also cost me in my relationship with my mother. I wouldn't speak to her about what I was going through, and I wouldn't allow her to speak life over me. It got to the point where she didn't even try to get me to open up anymore, since I had pushed her away so many times.

I thought that no one could give me justice. I had so many daydreams of exacting revenge against my abuser. I had no desire to hurt anyone but him.

But here's the reality: you might want the person who wronged you to be the sole focus of your fury and mistrust, but it spreads to everyone around you. Everyone gets tarred with the darkness of it. No relationship is spared.

That's why now, at thirty-eight, having everything that I have, having known being rich and being poor, I see that the Rosie I am today is about connection, relationship, and intimacy. Those are some of God's greatest gifts to us in this human experience, and I'm ready to reclaim that ground, whether or not I ever see a level of vindication. I have started to repair damaged relationships, beginning with my parents and then my brothers.

I won't allow injustice to continue to steal from me. And I don't want it to steal from you anymore either.

## STAY ON TOP OF IT

I have some good news about quicksand—really. As it turns out, it's quite possible to survive wandering into a quicksand trap. I know, I know. That sort of takes the fear out of those old movies I used to see. It's actually pretty hard to drown in quicksand.[2] Because of the amount of water needed to create quicksand, the human body will float in it, as long as said human is not flailing around. Quicksand can trap people when they find themselves sinking and they begin to panic, kicking and screaming, sending themselves deeper and deeper into the pit.

That was me in the years following the original abuse and in the years following other assaults I endured. I wandered into a pit of behaviors that I thought might protect me, numb me, and disprove the lies the abuse had instilled in me. I flailed around in that pit for a very long time, exposing myself to all kinds of further hurts and dangers. To this day, I still have to be on guard that I don't thrash around in a desperate attempt to find footing to even the score.

But I know more strongly than ever today that God's Word is true. Remember the story of Nabal and David I told you about earlier, and how Nabal self-destructed in the wake of an unrealized revenge against David? That same David went on to write these words about quicksand and rescue in Psalm 40:2:

> He lifted me out of the slimy pit,
>> out of the mud and mire;

he set my feet on a rock

and gave me a firm place to stand.

We learn later in that same chapter, in verse 14, that those who came against David, those who mocked him and hurt him and threatened him, hadn't come to justice—yet. But David had already been lifted out of that slimy pit. The God of grace had already given him a solid place to stand. That's what he's done for me and for you too.

Here's a profound truth: you don't have to hurt the people who hurt you to get your victory. You don't have to see them come to justice to claim your freedom. Your victory has already been secured. Your freedom has already been paid for. Stay on the path that moves you toward God, not the muddy, slimy trail of hurting those who have hurt you.

When it comes to the hurts we endure, the potential for a quicksand skinny-dip is all around us. But we have a God who is more than able to pull us free. Don't buy the lie that your freedom can come only when your enemy pays restitution. Jesus has already paid your ransom, and you don't have to live the quicksand life anymore. Set your feet, your hopes, and your future on the Rock: "For [God's people] drank from the spiritual rock that accompanied them, and that rock was Christ" (1 Cor. 10:4).

## BEFORE WE MOVE ON

1. What are some things you have done in response to the hurts you've experienced that, in turn, have hurt you?
2. Are you ready to exit that Quicksand of Self-Destruction? What would that look like?
3. Who could help you find the accountability and resources you might need to move forward?

*six*

# THE PITFALL OF WINDMILLS

HIS NAME WAS ALONSO QUIXANO, AND HE LOVED romance novels. As in, *really* loved them. Read them all the time. Soaked them up, invested his heart and attention in them. But these weren't just any romance novels; these were books that included all kinds of crazy adventures and mythical enemies and supernatural wonders. The romance novels we think of usually have a woman as the central character, but the romance novels Alonso was reading typically had a guy as the main character, a guy who would do anything for the woman he loved, who would endure any trial and go to any extreme to prove his love and protect her from a chaotic world.

Over time, Alonso began to live more in the fantasy of the books he was reading than in the real world of his boring day-to-day. He changed his name and left his hometown and his job. He began seeing intrigue around every corner. Soon he was living completely in a world of his own making, in which a hotel maid was a princess and the night clerk knighted Alonso. He fell in love with a girl from the rough side of town, believing her to be a duchess.

Ultimately, Alonso realized that all he had fought for, all the monsters he had vanquished, all the damsels he had rescued, had been for nothing. He died a defeated, disillusioned guy. His journey of romantic idealism and chivalrous vengeance led him to a destination of defeat in his inner man.

Great story, huh?

It actually is. Called the first modern novel, it's the work of the Spanish writer Miguel de Cervantes. In 1605, he published the first part of *The Ingenious Gentleman Don Quixote of La Mancha*, better known as *Don Quixote*. In the book, Alonso Quixano does a deep dive into stories of chivalry and intrigue, loses his grip on reality, and begins living out his life as a knight-errant, taking on the name of Don Quixote. Many consider Miguel de Cervantes one of the best writers in history, and his beautiful use of Castilian Spanish in his writing is something we Latinos continue to be proud of today. The novel has been translated into numerous languages and made into a hit Broadway musical. Its influence has even been credited in later great works.

Don Quixote is famous for fighting windmills. In his mind, the windmills that dotted the Spanish countryside were dragons—and there were windmills *everywhere* on his journey. He fought them ferociously with his lance. Sometimes he won, and sometimes he lost when his lance became caught in the blades of the windmill, and the force knocked him down.

*Don Quixote* is where the phrase "tilting at windmills" comes from. It means to see something as a foe, a big deal, an adversary, when it really isn't. It's when we allow something to be out of proportion with what it really is. It is when we struggle to see something as it really is and instead elevate it to a mythical, dragon-like presence.

I can be an Olympic-level windmill tilter. If you've ever experienced disappointment, betrayal, loss, upset (which we all have, in various intensities and degrees), then you might be at risk of windmill tilting too.

## WHEN A VANITY IS NOT JUST VANITY

Remember the entire home-renovation issue that I stopped feeding my husband over? Girl, I'm telling you, I'll never forget. After the intense conversations with our contractor, I'm amazed there was a contractor left in Los Angeles who was willing to speak to me. My husband oversaw a lot of the tradesmen, and we made a lot of decisions together. We'd start out needing to make a decision about something like flooring. At first glance, I'd feel kind of neutral about it. I'd gesture toward a couple of different tile choices and then tell Abel, "Pick which one you like." He would, and the floor would be installed, and then—wait for it—I wouldn't like it.

Listen, *I'm* shaking my head at myself. You don't need to do it too.

I made a superhuge deal about one aspect of the renovation, in particular, one thing I was really, really excited about from the start. As I've mentioned, I love beauty, cosmetics, and fashion—they're a big part of several of my businesses, and I'm personally into them as well. I love the process of putting on my makeup in the mornings, and I adore feeling feminine and girly and creative in putting together my personal look.

So I wanted the vanity of my dreams built for me.

You know the kind I'm talking about, right? A sit-down vanity with gorgeous cabinets and plenty of drawers to hold all my lotions and potions. The kind with the huge mirror framed with plenty of dressing-room-worthy lights. I wanted it in a big walk-in closet, where all my shoes and purses and outfits would be organized by color and style. I even knew the kind of beautiful chair I wanted in front of that vanity and mirror—one that looked like a little throne, wrapped in satin, fit for a wannabe beauty queen.

Part of the vision of that vanity was this: I wanted the whole thing to be white, from the vanity itself to the walls and flooring to that beautiful satin chair. Give me *all* the white finishes.

Abel was devoted to making my dream come true, and he oversaw all things vanity. One day he asked me about the paint finishes. "All white," I told him. "Everything white. That's what I want."

He gave me a big smile and said, "Can do!"

A few days later, I got a sneak peek of the project. Abel ushered me into the space to see the progress. I looked around, delighted at all the drawers and cabinets, the rows of dressing-room orb lights framing the big mirror, the vanity's perfect position in my big closet. It was all exciting. I had just one question.

"When's the paint coming in?"

"That's the paint," Abel replied, gesturing to the top of the vanity and the cabinet fronts. "White, like you said."

No. No, no, no.

It was matte paint. Flat. No sheen or shine to it. I thought it was the primer, not the final coat. But no, according to Abel, this was the final coat of paint. This wasn't a sneak peek; this was the final unveiling.

Oh dear.

Here's something important you need to know about me: I am a grade-A klutz. I'm the girl who can dribble some kind of food substance on her shirt within two minutes of putting on said shirt. I'm superclumsy. I consistently knock over my coffee, spill my shampoo, drop my eye shadow palettes. I kid you not—I've arrived at a meeting where someone spotted a little bit of fruit in my hair. Fruit in my hair? How did that happen? How is that a thing?

So when I saw the surface of that vanity with its matte finish, I knew that in no time I would stain, scuff, and otherwise ruin it.

I'm not justifying my response to the paint situation as rational. I'm just telling you how it went down.

I desperately didn't want to hurt Abel's feelings. After all, I was the one who gave him the admittedly vague instructions to paint everything white, without any mention of how I wanted everything glossy so that I could more easily wipe it all down. Instead, I just silently stressed over it. I'd sit down at that beautiful vanity to do my makeup and try to weirdly not touch anything while applying my blush or brushing on my mascara. It got to the point that I ultimately wouldn't even use it; instead I'd sit perched on the bathroom counter, makeup in my lap, twisting my face at a weird angle to the bathroom mirror, while that beautiful vanity sat unused just a few feet from me.

*¡Trágame tierra!* (That's frustrated Spanish for "Just let the earth swallow me up." I told you I was a tiny bit dramatic.)

Girl, I'm usually pretty laid-back about stuff like this. I figure I can just spray a little 409 on something and get it back to a pretty clean standard. But something about this whole vanity thing wore on me. It made me want to cry, it occupied my thoughts, and it changed the way I got ready for work every day.

It's not something I'm proud of. By focusing on the paint finish, I was missing so much of the bigger picture. The floors in my closet and around the vanity? Gorgeous. The overall work in the house following the renovation? Spectacular. But I was missing the celebration of what had been accomplished by allowing this one detail to become something it wasn't. I had turned the vanity paint job into the most important detail in the whole home reno.

## ISSUE DYSMORPHIA

I find the news stories that pop up on occasion about crazy lawsuits fascinating. There's one that is pretty much a poster child for this kind of thing. A judge in the Washington, DC, area went to pick up his dress slacks from the dry cleaner and found they had accidentally sent his pants home with the wrong person. They apologized for the mistake, tracked down the slacks, and returned them to the judge. He, in turn, decided to sue them for $67 million! The dry cleaner had a sign up in their shop that said "Satisfaction guaranteed," and the judge claimed that in misplacing his pants, they had violated their guarantee of satisfaction and therefore owed him millions and millions of dollars.[1]

Ultimately, the lawsuit was dismissed, but not after costing a whole lot of people, the dry cleaner included, a lot of time and money in legal fees. Something as small as a forty-dollar pair of pants turned into a huge ordeal all because of where that judge decided to put his focus.

Every time I drive my car, I see those words stamped onto the passenger-side mirror: "Objects in mirror are closer than they appear." It's a warning that my perception of how close or far another car might be can be off, particularly when I get ready to change lanes.

I think we sometimes suffer from miscalculating the actual scale of an issue. We minimize something that should be a big deal, or we can turn a small issue into something much larger. Like a pair of pants lost at the dry cleaner or a vanity not painted in a high-gloss finish.

Maybe you've experienced someone not greeting you when you walked into a meeting or a gathering. Did you start to fill in the blanks? *She didn't talk to me—I bet she's been talking behind my back, trying to bad-mouth me to other people. It's probably because I had that idea at the last meeting that she wasn't fully on board with. She's trying to discredit me. She probably thinks all my ideas are stupid. Or maybe she's intimidated by me. Yeah, I bet that's it. And now she's going to be all catty and rude. I can just tell . . .*

The reality is, you don't know why that woman didn't acknowledge you when you walked into the room. You don't know if she's truly giving you the evil eye or just got something under her contact lens. But you've expanded your assumption until it outsizes everything else that may have gone right in that meeting.

I've been most at risk of issue dysmorphia when it comes to a hurt or a slight or a wrong committed against me, particularly because my history and background include some legitimately huge injustices. You know how when you accidentally bite the inside of your cheek? That initial injury hurts like crazy and is a valid wound. But then if you hit that place again when you're eating dinner—even if you just graze the spot—it can hurt just as much or more than the original injury.

That's how it goes for me sometimes. It's like I'm now hyperaware of anything that feels off or wrong or upsetting. The danger to me, and to you, is that if we can't keep in perspective the day-to-day hurts and hassles, we feel like we're always under attack, always wounded, always outraged for justice to be done for every little thing. We can lose the value of relationships because we let little irritations turn into big issues. When we assign the same importance to everything and allow every wrong in our lives to carry the same weight and grief, we stand to lose what perspective would gain us: a greater peace and a greater grace for those in our lives.

## WHAT DOES A WINDMILL COST YOU?

Once upon a time, there was a kid who was the very definition of entitled. His father had had financial success, and the son was all about living the trust-fund-baby lifestyle. He demanded his portion of the family fortune, and his dad decided to go ahead and give it to him. The son took off, living the life of the ultimate Instagram influencer, renting the yachts, going to the exotic locales, paying everyone's bar tabs.

Now, this trust-fund baby had an older brother who stayed with the family business while his baby brother was out gallivanting around. He stayed loyal, he did the right things, he made sure details were covered and kept the taxes current. Then came the day when his younger brother showed back up on the doorstep, pockets empty, arrogance spent, head hanging. And his dad seemed totally cool with it.

Of course, this isn't a story I came up with. It's one that Jesus told, and it's recorded in the Gospels in the book of Luke. I've often heard this story come up in sermons, and a lot of the focus is on the father's response to the prodigal son returning home—the father's grace toward him. But I've always been interested in the older brother and his response to his brother's return. When the older brother discovered that a homecoming party, complete with great food and music, was underway for his younger brother, he "became angry and refused to go in" (Luke 15:28).

I get why the older brother wasn't thrilled with the party. I get why he would have much rather seen some kind of punishment carried out against his brother for his lack of maturity and for the grief he had caused the family. But the older brother allowed his perspective to cause him to miss an important moment. His father was joyful and elated. His brother was humbled and grateful. Yes, the older brother had a right to feel a little slighted, a little frustrated. But was anything gained by refusing to celebrate his brother's return and enjoy his father's elation?

Nope.

It didn't actually make the older brother feel better. It didn't mend the relationship with his younger brother. It didn't fix anything, resolve anything, or make anything even. The father then used the same kind of mercy and kindness with the older son when he acted like something of a spoiled brat that he used with the younger son when he returned. I mean, really, if the brother wanted "justice" for the younger brother's behavior, then he should have been ready to receive "justice" for his behavior in refusing to attend a party his father was giving. We can't love and desire justice only when it's pointed at other people. I surely want the mercy and grace of God extended to me. And yet, so often, I've wanted a heavy-handed justice against people who have slighted me. You can't want justice only when it works for you.

Are there some big wrongs in the world that should carry heavy consequences? Of course. But are there smaller wrongs that might not need the kind of due process that makes us feel better? Might our feelings about those issues be out of proportion? Well, yeah.

Compromise can be valid, you know. A compromise is where everyone wins and loses, and sometimes that's the best way.

For the older brother in Luke 15, what would a compromise have looked like? How would that situation have looked in proportion?

Well, he could have showed up for the homecoming party. And later, privately, he could have had a heart-to-heart with his dad about feeling let down that his faithfulness didn't seem to be as celebrated as his brother's return. See, it's not wrong to acknowledge how something has made you feel. But it's problematic when you make something all about you when a response of that magnitude isn't needed.

# CHASING DRAGONS INSTEAD OF DREAMS

When I look at the fictional story of Don Quixote, I have to wonder, what did he hope to achieve by attacking those windmills he had reimagined as dragons? Part of the answer lies in the story itself; he was definitely trying to attract the attention of the chick he was crushing on. But what else was motivating him?

That's a question I've had to ask myself when I've been tilting at my own windmills. What am I trying to prove? And to whom?

Look, I believe there is absolutely a time to pursue justice. But I also think we've got to be clear about our motives. Chasing anything costs us time. Time is a precious commodity this side of heaven. Since the price you're paying for anything is time, you better make sure it's worth it. At the end of the day, a windmill, even when perceived as a dragon, isn't going to hurt anyone.

I have chased windmills because I wanted to prove to other people that I was right. I have chased windmills to prove that I wasn't wrong. And I have chased windmills simply because I didn't want life to be the way it was.

I'm all about pursuing the most vibrant, best life God has for us. But as believers in Jesus, we must look at the world the way it truly is. And once we see how it really is, then we can help create change. There are absolutely "dragons" worth fighting. And there are windmills that are just . . . windmills.

I think about Gideon in the book of Judges. He was living in an oppressed environment, with the Israelites' enemy, the Midianites, marauding and attacking towns throughout the region. Gideon famously hid in a winepress to thresh wheat, because he was afraid that enemy forces would spot him. An angel encountered him there and told him that he would be the one to lead in driving back the enemy. Gideon asked for three signs to verify this call on his life, which God answered; then Gideon gathered an army and headed out to attack the enemy.

What I love in this story is that Gideon was not unrealistic about the enemy he would be facing in battle. He didn't go looking for a fight, but he allowed the Lord to prepare him. And his story helps me better understand the way God will speak to me and use me in a fight when he is my Defender:

1. **Gideon was more than aware that the Midianites were a horrific foe.** It isn't wrong to understand the power of your enemy; as a matter of fact, I would say it is critical to be realistic about what you're up against. Gideon would not have been able to take on such a powerful foe alone. That's why he was hiding in the winepress, out of a good understanding of just what was going on for his country. But we sometimes get confused and make enemies out of things that aren't and allow true enemies to have a place in our lives. Worse still, we sometimes refuse to acknowledge things that are truly dangerous to us, thinking that it wouldn't be "faith" to see them as such. Gideon's example teaches me that recognizing real dragons is critical to seeing what God can do.

2. **Gideon let God verify the call on his life.** I know, I know. Sometimes Bible teachers will use the story of Gideon and his request for signs from God to show his nervousness or lack of faith. When the angel told Gideon that he would lead in battle, Gideon asked for three signs: for the angel to wait for him to bring a sacrifice; for a sheep's fleece to first be wet and the ground around the fleece to be dry; and then the next night, for the fleece to be dry and the ground to be wet. See, sometimes I want to head out into a fight that is not mine. I don't think it's always a lack of faith to ask God to verify your assignment; I'd call it wise. You may see wrongs out there in the world that absolutely are your assignment to fight, with God leading. And there may be

skirmishes you feel you should jump into, but they're not meant for you. Cooperating with God as your Defender means listening carefully for the battles he equips you for and the battles he excuses you from.

3. **Gideon did battle God's way.** Gideon started out with a great battle plan. He had 32,000 men willing to go with him against the enemy. But the Midianite army numbered 135,000, meaning that Gideon's men were outnumbered by more than four to one. It *is* a great testimony to the kind of leadership Gideon exhibited to be able to rally that number of men to go up against such difficult odds. But God had a different kind of fight in mind. God told Gideon to *reduce* the number of his army.

See, Gideon started out wanting to fight just like the enemy would: more men, more swords. But when God calls you to do battle, he might have you use far different tactics than what you're seeing from the opposing side. He may call you to use prayer. He may call you to use fasting. He may call you to use compassion. He may call you to use Scripture. He for sure tells you not to use gossip or slander or hatefulness. But that's the genius of what God does when he calls you into a fight. He's not bound by the usual battle tactics.

4. **Gideon kept checking in to make sure he was on the right path.** After Gideon had rallied the army that God had him trim down to just 300 guys, God did this for Gideon: "During that night the LORD said to Gideon, 'Get up, go down against the [enemy] camp, because I am going to give it into your hands. If you are afraid to attack, go down to the camp with your servant Purah and listen to what they are saying. Afterward, you will be encouraged to attack the camp'" (Judg. 7:9–11). Gideon obeyed. He snuck down to the enemy camp and overheard a couple of guys talking about a weird dream one of them had. Gideon knew

exactly what it meant, and he came back to his men encouraged about the course they were taking, even with being outrageously outnumbered in men and weapons.

I love that Gideon went down to the enemy camp to hear what they were saying. I love that he didn't respond to the Lord's prompting with "I got it, I got it, Lord. I'm so full of faith, I don't need your encouragement." No, Gideon remained humble, and he was willing to continue receiving God's encouragement and confirmation.

Here's the lesson for you and me: we need to keep checking in with God when it comes to confronting the hurts and challenges in our lives. He is faithful to confirm our path. If we decide we don't need to hear from him for a while, that we've got this battle plan down cold, then we're in deep danger.

5. There was no "brag" at the end. Sometimes, when we come through a battle, when the people who hurt us get what's coming to them and the consequences of their behavior catch up with them, we can be tempted to pat ourselves on the back for righting a wrong. But God had specific reasons for reducing Gideon's army the way he did. Check out Judges 7:2: "The LORD said to Gideon, 'You have too many men. I cannot deliver Midian into their hands, or Israel would boast against me, "My own strength has saved me."'" Look, we sometimes want to go tilting after windmills so that we can have personal bragging rights about taking down someone who has hurt others, who has treated customers unethically, or who has been a thorn in the side of the community. But when God is our Defender and we are walking closely with him, we should always know that any victory over evil is due to him. If you feel called into a fight, check your language. Is it about how smart you were to figure out where the breach in HR occurred? Do you talk about your sparkling

detective skills in determining how someone violated a contract? Or do you give glory to God that he has allowed you to help play a part in making something right?

Riding into a battle can feel noble. And sometimes it is. But when I think about Don Quixote, I'm reminded that in the quest of understanding God as my Defender, I want to make sure I'm dialed into what is a true fight and a true cause God wants me to take on, and what might just be my idealism or identity talking. Who am I really trying to be in these situations? What am I really fighting? Am I making every windmill a dragon? These are the questions I need to ask myself so I won't stay locked in a battle over every single thing I perceive to be a slight or a side-eye or a snicker. There are fights worth fighting. And there are fights solely of my own perception. Knowing the difference is an important step on the journey toward knowing that God is my Defender.

## BEFORE WE MOVE ON

1. What fights have you been passionate about that ended up not actually being what you thought they were?

2. What are some ways God has instructed you to do battle that don't make sense when you see what your opponent is up to?

3. Do prayer, fasting, compassion, and Scripture feel like "weapons" to you? Or do you sometimes think people can use those things as an excuse to do nothing? Why do you feel this way?

*seven*

# THE RAVINE OF VINDICATION

HE HAD SOME TIME ON HIS HANDS, SO HE DECIDED
to write.

John first had a career in making and selling custom cookware. He had learned the business from his father and had developed a franchise of his own. He got married, had a baby, and was living a pretty typical life.

Until a deep passion took hold of him.

John began to read more intently in the Word of God. He also encountered some teaching about leading a life fully devoted to Jesus. It changed everything.

He was living in a country where, through a series of political changes, restrictions were put on what he could say and believe about his relationship with God. The government set limits on how the faith community could gather together to worship and celebrate their beliefs. But because of what John had experienced in his walk with God, he felt he had no choice but to stand for what he believed in, even if it meant there would be serious repercussions.

There were.

John was arrested and thrown in prison. That's why he had some time on his hands. That's why he decided to write.

Little did he know at the time that the writing he composed during his time in jail would become the first novel published in English. Little did he know that over the next 340 years, his book would never be out of print. Little did he know that this novel would be translated into more than two hundred languages. Little did he know the impact his book would have.

But God knew.

*The Pilgrim's Progress*, written in 1678 by the cookware-salesman-turned-passionate-preacher John Bunyan, is one of the most beloved stories in Christian literature. It's the story of a man named Christian who was making his way from the City of Destruction to the Celestial City. He carried on his back the burden of his own sins and failings. He met many characters along the way, some who helped him in his journey and others who attempted to throw him off course. He also passed through many places, or stations, along the way—places that could have thrown him off course, places where he could have become stuck, and places that tempted him to turn around and go back home.

But Christian persevered through it all with divine help.

One of the parts of the story I love most is all the stations that Christian must pass through to arrive at the Celestial City. Each of these stops is a place I've struggled through in my own journey of faith. That's partly why I talk about seeing God as our Defender as a journey we undergo that has its own perils and possible pitfalls. It's an allegory, a story with real-world applications, that I pray will help us all navigate the wrongs we have suffered.

In this journey toward seeing God as our Defender, I believe there is a dangerous ravine reminiscent of some of the places Christian had to pass through in *The Pilgrim's Progress*. We must make our way through the Ravine of Vindication to find greater freedom. The trick is that this gorge can seem like a place where you can find a lot of healing. When you first enter it, things seem to brighten up as the sunshine brings light to the dark corners of your soul.

But no ravine experiences full sunshine. The embrace of the

cliffs on both sides can render the valley floor a study in shades of gray. On one side, soaring into the heights, is that which is good. On the other side, hovering darkly, is that which is wrong and evil. In between, we traverse a landscape that seems like a confusing blend of both at times as we enter the chasm seeking vindication. I love this imagery.

Vindication is when you not only want the person who wronged you to be exposed, but you also want to prove that you were right, that you were not to blame in the situation. Hear me well: this is a dangerous, treacherous place.

It's dangerous for two reasons, two deadly games.

## THE SHAME GAME

First, we have a culture that tends to blame victims in horrifically unfair ways. Sociologists and psychologists tell us there is often a prejudice against victims. It's part of the way we try to insulate ourselves from the fear that the same thing could happen to us.[1] "Well, you should have seen what she was wearing that night," the judgmental classmate will say. "Of course, no one has any business being in that part of town," a gossipy neighbor will say. "If it looks too good to be true, then it is," a self-congratulatory business colleague will say about a peer who got fleeced in an ill-fated partnership.

Victimology is the study of how and why victims are blamed, and it reveals that victims of domestic and sexual abuse are most often the targets of victim blaming. But victim blaming is not exclusive to those situations. It can happen in situations of extortion, and it can happen in emotional contexts as well. Whether it occurs by saying the victim shares responsibility for the attack or by casting doubt on a victim when she or he comes forward, it causes incredible pain for those who experience it.

Victim blaming leverages the shame of what happened and acts as if the person who suffered the hurt should have known better, figured out how to avoid the situation, or done something in the moment to stop what was happening.

I've had people bring the shame game against me, and I've brought it against myself. For me, that was one of the most dangerous parts of the journey toward vindication.

When I discovered that the extended family member who sexually abused me had gone on to abuse my niece, I was tormented with guilt. I had not spoken up about the abuse I experienced until I discovered what he was doing to her. In my mind, I was responsible for what had happened to her. Never mind that I was still a kid myself and terrified of the perpetrator. That guilt became the burden on my back as I stumbled my way toward allowing God to be my Defender. I would carry it for years.

At the trial to prosecute this pedophile, I found such relief from the judge overseeing the case. The *Press-Telegram* reported:

Rivera's sister, Rosa, also addressed the court, saying that, because of Marin, she had lost her innocence at age 8. For years afterward, she said, she also lost her trust "in men, herself and the world."

As for a proper sentence for the defendant, she said, she couldn't offer an opinion.

"I don't know what a person's childhood is worth," she said.

Rosa Rivera also told the judge that she could no longer look her niece "in the eyes" because of her own lingering guilt.

Had she reported the abuse immediately, she said, her niece might never have been victimized.

Interjecting, [Judge] Comparet-Cassani told Rivera that all the guilt belonged to Marin—not to her.

"You are not responsible for anything that happened," she said.

Rosa Rivera nodded, and said, "Thank you."[2]

To have someone in authority, someone who understood and upheld the law, tell me that I didn't need to carry this guilt any longer alleviated a heaviness that had been with me for so long.

To those who like to think the Bible is a collection of children's stories with simple outcomes, I would say, "Go actually read Scripture!" The Bible has complex accounts of the messiness of people's lives. One of the toughest reads to me is the story of Tamar.

Tamar was one of King David's daughters. She was a great beauty. King David had several wives, even though God's Word had advised against a ruler taking a number of wives. David had numerous children by all these wives, and Tamar was his daughter with his wife Maakah. They also had a son together named Absalom.

Now, David had another son, Amnon, by his wife Ahinoam. Amnon became obsessed with his half sister Tamar. Sometimes you'll read a translation of 2 Samuel 13:2 that makes it sound as if Amnon was in love with Tamar. Nope. That's not what the original language says. In the original Hebrew in verse 2, it says that he was so distressed by not being able to find a way to sleep with her that he literally made himself sick. That's not lovesick. That's just a sick that the Bible calls lust.

Amnon turned to his cousin Jonadab for advice, and Jonadab recommended the following course of action:

> "Go to bed and pretend to be ill," Jonadab said. "When your father comes to see you, say to him, 'I would like my sister Tamar to come and give me something to eat. Let her prepare the food in my sight so I may watch her and then eat it from her hand.'" (2 Sam. 13:5)

Now, I want to give Jonadab a little benefit of the doubt. Maybe his intent was just to get Amnon some face time with Tamar and some sympathy from her. It's still bad advice, given that Amnon had no business pursuing any kind of intimate relationship with Tamar. But maybe Jonadab wasn't thinking that Amnon would take it as far as he did.

Amnon did as Jonadab recommended and asked his father, David, to tell Tamar to go check on her half brother. When Tamar did, Amnon's true intentions became known. He raped her and then told her to get out. His obsession spent, he didn't want anything more to do with her. This was not love; this was a crime, and it is important as people reading God's Word that we don't engage in trying to rewrite this as a love story gone wrong. It was a crime, plain and simple.

Tamar was shattered. The Word says,

> Tamar put ashes on her head and tore the ornate robe she was wearing. She put her hands on her head and went away, weeping aloud as she went. Her brother Absalom said to her, "Has that Amnon, your brother, been with you? Be quiet for now, my sister; he is your brother. Don't take this thing to heart."

And Tamar lived in her brother Absalom's house, a desolate woman. (2 Sam. 13:19–20)

Those are some loaded sentences. Absalom minimized her heartbreak and told her to be silent about what had happened to her. She lived as a "desolate woman." The Hebrew word for "desolate," *shamem*, is also translated "destroyed."

Friend, don't miss this. Tamar had done nothing wrong. But the shame she felt, the burden she carried for it, shattered her. This is the last we hear of her. She collapsed to the floor of this deep ravine and stayed there.

Likewise, the hurt you have experienced—not necessarily the person who committed the hurt, but the hurt itself—is out to destroy you. One of the ways it will seek to do that is through the shame game.

You might think that you are the one to blame for what happened, like Tamar did. Shame can keep you from seeing things as they really are. Victim blaming gets turned inward. Somehow you believe you are responsible.

The money that was stolen from your account by a person you trusted? You might say things to yourself like *I was too trusting. I should have seen the signs.*

That boss who rages and threatens and bullies? You might be thinking, *Well, if I could only get more work done and not be so sensitive, then it would be okay.*

That guy you've been dating who has smacked you around a couple of times? *I provoked him*, you may tell yourself. *He's supersweet almost all of the time. I just need to not make him mad like that again.*

Sister, please. We must not allow the shadows of the Ravine

of Vindication to overtake us. There are situations in which you might have responsibility, and we'll get to those a little later in the chapter. But there are situations in which you do not. Your one responsibility is to trust God to lead you through this place. That's it. You don't have to try to rehabilitate your abuser. You don't have to keep secrets that your family would prefer you not tell. You don't have to make excuses for the business partner who blew it. You don't have to make excuses, because their behaviors are their responsibility, not yours.

What if continuing to shoulder a blame that is not yours to carry only prolongs the time until God deals with your abuser and justice is served? I'm not telling you to let go of the shame to exact revenge, but I am telling you that when you allow God to be your Defender, you no longer hide in the shadows, carrying a shame that is not yours to own. Look at this beautiful promise:

> "Fear not, for you will not be put to shame;
> And do not feel humiliated, for you will not be disgraced;
> But you will forget the shame of your youth."
> (Isa. 54:4 NASB)

In these situations, you were wronged, thoroughly wronged, and therefore, you are in the right. It's the right kind of right. Next, we'll look at the wrong kind of right as we journey through the Ravine of Vindication.

## THE BLAME GAME

The Ravine of Vindication is also a dangerous place because it's possible to convince ourselves that we had no responsibility for what happened. As we just discussed, there are situations in which someone is purely the victim. But when we look to be right about just how wronged we were, there are times we have to own our part.

A friend of mine counsels a lot of married couples who are in crisis. She says the Ravine of Vindication is the place where marriages are either healed or completely come apart. Couples who are in deep distress arrive at her counseling couch and begin their narrative. Often, one spouse feels that the other is entirely at fault. That spouse will have a long list of everything that has gone wrong and how the other person is to blame. This is only heightened if one of the spouses does seem more "guilty"—for example, if he or she had an affair or has an addiction.

Sometimes it's true—one person in the relationship has completely blown the thing up. But my friend says that what is fascinating in many of these cases is that there is generally a pattern of behavior between the two partners that has led to these more glaring transgressions on the part of one of them.

Okay, now stay with me. I know that could make you mad. But it's important. You still here? Good.

What she means is this: when we have been hurt, it's very easy to see the action that person took that is wrong. We can clearly call out the event that broke our hearts, betrayed our trust, or stabbed us in the back.

What is harder is evaluating whether we had a part in it, and in what proportion, and then owning it.

For example, let's take a situation in which a wife has an affair. Is she wrong for stepping outside her marriage vows? One hundred percent. Are there cases in which a marriage was happy and healthy until one of the partners made a series of poor choices to pursue a flirtation? Yep. But according to my friend, you don't see that a lot: a marriage that is happy and healthy going sideways out of the blue. More often, she tells me, a series of events happen on the part of both spouses. The wife communicates to her spouse that she has a love language, and he thinks all that is silly. Or she has asked for his romantic attention, and he can't be bothered. Or his temper has been an issue. When temptation comes—and it will, because that's how the Enemy works—the wife lets that neglect or hurt feeling or unexpressed upset become the launch pad for trying to find wholeness in another romance.

I am in no way saying the wife is justified in straying. I am in no way trying to blame her moral choices on her husband. But I am saying the issues are layered. They go deeper. In this case, if the husband is seeking vindication, believing that he alone is the wronged party, the future of the marriage is bleak. Likewise, if the wife tries to defend the affair by cataloging her husband's behavior, also engaging in a form of vindication, then the odds are slim that this couple will make it out of the ravine intact.

I think the Ravine of Vindication is where brothers Jacob and Esau lived for a long time, each of them hurling threats and ultimatums. They were fraternal twins and lived up to that designation. They were very different people who happened to be born at the same time. Esau was known as an outdoorsman, and Jacob was more of a homebody. Esau had a more impetuous nature, and Jacob was more strategic. Those differences played out dramatically when Jacob, with the help of his mother, Rebekah, helped trick Esau out of his birthright as oldest son. Jacob ended up fleeing his hometown because of Esau's fury over the situation. Genesis 27:41 records Esau's response: "Esau held a grudge against Jacob because of the blessing his father had given him. He said to himself, 'The days of mourning for my father are near; then I will kill my brother Jacob.'"

Initially, to my legal mind and my strong sense of fair and unfair, this seems to be an open-and-shut case. Jacob and his mom, Rebekah, absolutely tricked Isaac, the blind, elderly father of Jacob and Esau, into giving Jacob the inheritance intended for his older brother. Case closed, right?

Ah, but wait.

When we track back a few chapters in Scripture, there is an early account between the brothers that makes the situation a little more complicated. One day when they were younger, Esau came in from hunting, famished and tired. He smelled the stew and bread his brother, Jacob, had been whipping up in the kitchen and demanded a bowl. Jacob exacted a promise out of him in exchange for lunch:

Jacob replied, "First sell me your birthright." "Look, I am about to die," Esau said. "What good is the birthright to me?" But Jacob said, "Swear to me first." So he swore an oath to him, selling his birthright to Jacob. Then Jacob gave Esau some bread and some lentil stew. He ate and drank, and then got up and left. So Esau despised his birthright. (Gen. 25:31–34)

I don't like this little stunt Jacob pulled any more than you do. But let's not miss that last verse: "So Esau despised his birthright."

We each have a birthright as children of God. But we sometimes don't value our birthright the way we should. We allow circumstances and conveniences to get in the way, and we cut corners, we whine, or we ignore. Then when someone swoops in and takes away what should have been ours, we cry, "They're to blame!" Or we justify our response because of their actions.

That's where Jacob and Esau ended up. Jacob realized that

Esau was hunting for him, so he had to pack up his whole life and head for the hills.

So the question we have to ask ourselves is this: *What is my responsibility in this situation?* Owning our responsibility doesn't always mean that things will be put back together. But it does mean that once we know, understand, and repent of our part in it, we will be free to move through this dangerous place and on to the brighter day God has for us, regardless of the other party's choices.

What became of Jacob and Esau?

From what we can tell from Scripture, they were divided by their animosity and fear for around twenty years. Jacob worked far from home for his father-in-law, Laban, all that time, but there came a point in their relationship when Jacob wanted to be his own man. He made plans to return to his homeland, but he knew it would involve entering the Ravine of Vindication.

Literally and figuratively.

As it turns out, the place where Jacob and Esau met after this long separation was a deep valley with a river running through it. That river, in biblical times, was called the Jabbok; today it is known as the Zarqa River. Jacob was scared to meet his twin for the first time in twenty years. As he prepared to go into Esau's territory, he spent a restless evening on one side of the Jabbok, with his wives and all his possessions on the other side. He was completely alone—and then he wasn't. He found himself wrestling with a mysterious man. This account is what would become the famous story of Jacob wrestling with God. After this encounter, God changed Jacob's name to Israel, and Jacob walked with a limp. As dawn turned to day, Jacob approached the area where he expected he would see Esau.

This was the moment. If this story were made into a movie,

the suspenseful music would be rising. Esau would approach from his side of the valley, walking to the banks of the river. And Jacob would tentatively approach from his side, unsure of what would come next.

Scripture says that Jacob "himself went on ahead and bowed down to the ground seven times as he approached his brother. But Esau ran to meet Jacob and embraced him; he threw his arms around his neck and kissed him. And they wept" (Gen. 33:3–4).

Jacob and Esau entered the Ravine of Vindication, in this case, that fierce, cavernous gorge holding the Jabbok. Jacob approached Esau with humility and honor. Esau approached Jacob with love and heart. They laid down the idea of trying to validate their own positions with regard to their original dispute and found vindication in being reunited.

To me, their reunion is a living example of what Paul would write to the church at Rome almost two thousand years later: "Do not repay anyone evil for evil. Be careful to do what is right in the eyes of everyone. If it is possible, as far as it depends on you, live at peace with everyone" (Rom. 12:17–18). Both Jacob and Esau would have been justified in continuing to hold their positions. They were both right: Esau should never have treated his inheritance with such casualness, and Jacob should never have enticed Esau to give it up. But they both would have been wrong in missing out on the rest of their years as loving and supportive brothers to each other.

What does all this mean for you and me? Girl, I have some things I've carried too much blame for. I've shouldered a burden of guilt far too long in situations where I had no responsibility for what happened. I've also placed too much blame on people in other situations in my life. I've been left for long seasons in the Ravine of Vindication, where the shadows have colored my life gray. There are important reasons for traveling through that gorge. We will have to wrestle with God to understand what part we might have played. We might come out of the ravine limping a bit, having discovered that we need to walk in humbleness to find wholeness. Or we might come out of the ravine feeling lighter, with a new perspective on what happened to us.

Press on, sister. Don't let the lessons of this sacred place pass you by. What is learned here is too precious not to take with you on the rest of the journey.

## BEFORE WE MOVE ON

1. What is something for which you may be carrying too much guilt?
2. What would allow you to lay that burden down?
3. What is a situation in which you have believed you had no responsibility, but the Holy Spirit is now convicting you that you have some amends to make?
4. Read Genesis 32:22–31. Notice that Jacob wrestled with God just before Jacob was to meet Esau for the first time in two decades. What did Jacob demand of the being he wrestled with? What did you learn about what you want to take with you into the Ravine of Vindication when it comes to confronting hurts from your past? How can God your Defender equip you for the experience?

*eight*

# THE TRAP OF AVOIDANCE

HERE'S SOMETHING I LIKE ABOUT MYSELF: I DON'T procrastinate.

I probably have my brother Juan to thank for that.

Okay, not completely. I've always liked getting my tasks done, making the grade, and hitting the deadline. But Juan certainly helped reinforce it.

Here's the thing about Juan: he and I are the babies of the family. He's the fourth of the five siblings and I'm the fifth, so he's the baby boy of the crew and I'm the baby girl. And I'm the Baby. As in, the true baby of the family. (I just had to throw that in there. It's important.)

Juan and I have always been close. I've always felt that Juan is the most brilliant of all the Rivera kids. He can fix anything, figure anything out, and remember all kinds of amazing things. He has a crazy work ethic like all of us Riveras do: work hard, work with excellence. But when it came to anything about school, he was lazy. L-A-Z-Y. He would never crack open a book, never study. He was always able to get by on his good looks, his charm, and his athletic ability.

Listen, I'm not gossiping about Juan here. He would tell you himself how lazy he was in school. Except it would probably take too much effort for him to tell you. I'm just here to help.

As Juan was finishing up high school, all he wanted to do was play baseball. He was (and is) a great ballplayer, and he didn't want his baseball days to be over. He decided to go to college so he could continue to play. For reasons I still can't understand, he signed up for eighteen units one semester. I was still in high school, but I knew he was going to be in over his head. I told him I didn't think taking eighteen units was a good idea. It was a full load and then some, and he still had baseball practice all the time, along with the game schedule. I didn't think Juan was really listening to me until he approached me with a plan.

One afternoon when we were both home, he said, "Rosie, here's what I need you to do. I'm going to sign up to take one of these classes online. Then you can just take it for me. You make As on everything. Studying is no big deal to you. You can take this class online as me, and I'll do the other fifteen units, and that will work great!"

Now, in my defense, this was said in passing. It wasn't as if we had a serious conference, signed paperwork, and agreed on a schedule. He seemed kind of serious and kind of not. I didn't really feel like clarifying just how much in the joke category this idea of his was. I procrastinated getting online and seeing what the course was about. I procrastinated looking at the assignments for the semester. I literally procrastinated everything possible for a virtual class.

Fast-forward four months. The end of the semester was just a handful of days away. I had done well in my high school courses and was diligently studying for my finals. I was at my dad's office one afternoon when Juan stopped by. He was proud of himself. For the first time ever, he was going to make really good grades in all his courses. And he'd done it while keeping up with a rigorous baseball schedule. He was giving my dad the good news when he turned to me and said, "Rosie, you finished up that online course for me, right?"

I froze—the deer-in-the-headlights kind of frozen. "Um . . ." I mumbled.

"What?" Juan demanded.

"I, uh, well . . ." Stammering seemed my best defense at the moment.

The reality was I had never even logged on to take a look at the course. I'd never watched one lecture, never turned in one assignment, never glanced at the syllabus.

"Rosie, what did you do?" Juan thundered.

I haltingly let him know that, um, no, "me posing as he" had never shown up for the virtual class.

Livid doesn't even begin to cover Juan's response. He yelled, hollered, threatened, yelled some more, and began to make menacing statements toward me. We faced off across my dad's desk, with Dad watching us, his head bobbing back and forth as if he were at a tennis match. I would make another excuse, and Juan would explode in a fresh way; I would make a defense, and Juan would counter. Back and forth this contest of college-course chaos raged.

I'd finally had enough and said, "It's not my fault! I'm leaving!" I grabbed my purse and fished out my keys; then I ran out of my dad's office for the parking lot. I hopped into my car, slammed the door, and skidded out of my parking spot, only to realize that Juan had jumped in his car and was tailing me.

Now I was freaked out! What was he going to do to me when he caught me? Was he going to yell at me some more or try to embarrass me in front of friends?

He followed me all the way home, about fifteen minutes away from my dad's office. I squealed into the driveway, threw my car into park, and dashed up to the front door before Juan could start yelling at me again in the front yard. I tore up to my room and locked the door. Juan came bellowing into the house, banging around and letting off steam.

After a couple of hours, we were pals again. That's how it works with Juan and me. The good news is, he managed to pass all his classes that semester and keep up his grades. I'm not exactly sure how that happened, but I know I didn't have anything to do with it, online or otherwise.

I learned that procrastination was not my friend. But it took me a few more years to understand the danger of a deeper kind of procrastination.

On the one hand, I had procrastinated in taking Juan's online class for him. But that wasn't the real procrastination issue. I had never planned on taking Juan's class, whether or not I thought he was joking. It would have been cheating. It wouldn't have been fair to him or to me. My high school schedule was plenty packed with Advanced Placement classes, and I didn't have time. It would have been lying for Juan, and I wasn't going to do that.

So what I truly procrastinated on was confronting the issue. I avoided going back to Juan and asking him if he was kidding or if this was his real expectation of me. I dodged getting that clarification because it could have led to us having a strong disagreement about the ethics of his baby sister impersonating him online. I evaded the confrontation because I didn't want him to be disappointed in me or think I wasn't being supportive of him.

That's the Trap of Avoidance. When we avoid certain issues in our journey of justice, when we procrastinate in facing the root of a hurt, we risk an even bigger injury down the road.

That's the danger of procrastination. We can think we're just too busy to deal with something. We don't have time. It's fine, it's fine. But procrastination issues aren't just about being "lazy" or distracted. Procrastination is avoidance, and the longer we put off dealing with the hurts and wrongs in our lives, the deeper the infection and decay to our sense of peace can go.

I can tell you from experience that avoiding dealing with the root of an issue allows the problem to spread beyond what you can imagine.

## A TIME TO TALK

This is where our journey takes an interesting turn as we continue learning how to lean into God as our Defender. Many of us need help with not trying to take matters into our own hands. We need help with not trying to get back at someone. We need to check our hearts and remind ourselves to let God determine the time, the place, and the manner in which he will come to our defense.

But some of us also have a tendency to let things go for too long. We stay silent when we should speak up. We neglect to call out that which has unrighteously crossed a boundary.

It can feel very subtle, the difference between wisely keeping our mouths shut about some things and appropriately exposing others. After all, there are verses that advise staying silent: "It is good to wait quietly for the salvation of the LORD" (Lam. 3:26) and "For God alone, O my soul, wait in silence, for my hope is from him" (Ps. 62:5 ESV) are just a couple. I've seen people use verses like these to avoid calling out an abuse or issue in their lives. I've done it myself. Let's face it: it can seem more comfortable to simply not say anything than to open up a can of worms. When we're wanting to walk well with God, it can almost feel more righteous or grace filled not to speak up.

But there are also verses that are very clear about our responsibility not to allow sinful behaviors to continue. Paul wrote, "Have nothing to do with the fruitless deeds of darkness, but rather expose them" (Eph. 5:11). A few verses later, Paul explained the necessity of calling out unfruitful deeds: "Everything exposed by the light becomes visible" (v. 13). There are times when it is essential to call out abuse, illegal acts, and the exploitation of the helpless. To speak up does not replace God as our Defender; it allows us to do battle alongside him. When we allow God to be our Defender, we do our part by speaking up about an evil offense against us; then we allow God to determine what happens next. Consider these words from John: "We accept human testimony, but God's testimony is greater because it is the testimony of God" (1 John 5:9).

I can practically hear you in my head. "But Rosie, what about 1 Peter 4:8? It says that 'love covers over a multitude of sins'! Shouldn't I just move on?"

It's a fair question. But here's where I think we get confused. We are mixing up the spats and hurt feelings that can come from differences of opinion and the friction of living alongside other humans with the behaviors and decisions that could harm, defraud, or put others at risk.

For example, my husband, Abel, and I can have some good old-fashioned arguments. He can make me so mad sometimes. But that's where my love for him should be activated as a cover. He's not making me mad out of a harmful spirit; we just don't happen to agree on something. Or let's say there's someone at church who strongly believes that we should offer a particular ministry class, and I don't. We each feel pretty passionately about it, and we might even have some hurt feelings toward each other. But at the end of the day, neither of us has any business going around spreading those feelings. That's gossip, and God's Word is full of warnings about this kind of speaking. That church colleague and I owe it to each other to cover what we consider each other's wrongs when it comes to differences of opinion and perspective.

But love should not cover a multitude of potentially victim-producing wrongs. Let's say I have a friend who is talking harshly against someone else. Now, I could avoid having a loving but confrontational conversation with my friend about the damage she could be doing to the other person and that person's reputation and heart. But if I put off that conversation, if I procrastinate in doing what is hard but right, I would be responsible for allowing another human being to potentially be hurt by my friend's gossip.

I take seriously this warning from the book of Ezekiel, even though it can be controversial or hard to understand:

> "[When] you do not warn [a wicked person] or speak out to dissuade them from their evil ways in order to save their life, that wicked person will die for their sin, and I will hold you accountable for their blood. But if you do warn the wicked person and they do not turn from their wickedness or from their evil ways, they will die for their sin; but you will have saved yourself." (3:18–19)

If I don't take action and I allow a gossip cycle to continue, I believe I carry a responsibility for that.

Some pretty alarming information is out there about pedophiles who continue to find their way into schools and children's church programs and youth groups. Why does this happen? Because organizations don't speak up.[1] They don't want to risk the reputation of their school or ministry or youth camp, so they cover up what has happened. Before you know it, the abuser has moved on to the next school, ministry, or youth camp. Love, true love, exposes these kinds of wrongs so they don't happen again. A misunderstanding of love hides these kinds of sins and evils, and in doing so allows the fungus to spread further.

I realize I've used examples that are one extreme or the other, a typical marital spat versus child abuse. Let's look at some situations that don't seem to fall clearly in one camp or the other. Imagine you become aware that a gal in your small group is talking behind your back. Right off the bat, this is tricky, because the way you typically would find this out is if someone comes to you and lets you know. There's a risk that you could be participating in the same thing she's doing, throwing around some gossipy hash that the Bible says goes down like Chick-fil-A nuggets. (No, really! Proverbs 18:8 and 26:22 both say, "The words of a gossip are like choice morsels; they go down to the inmost parts." "Choice morsels" in my book taste like Chick-fil-A nuggets!)

A friend of mine had something like this happen. Several years ago, her husband was offered a full-time position at their church. After a lot of prayer and discussion, they felt that he was not supposed to accept the position, but rather that he was supposed to stay in his "secular" job. (By the way, for what it's worth, I believe the Word of God teaches us that all work done as unto the Lord is sacred, whether that's on a ministry staff or not.) They were honored but politely declined the offer. A member of their congregation began telling other members of the congregation that the reason my friend and her husband had turned it down was because he made more money in his secular job. She went on to question their decision, claiming that it was terrible that they were ignoring a call of God on their lives because of money. Because this person was someone my friend and her husband had considered a friend, other members of the congregation assumed this information was correct, that this person must have gotten the reason directly from my friend.

However, that wasn't the case. My friend had never said anything like that, and finances weren't the reason. As a matter of fact, the ministry position would have been more financially stable for them. My friend and her husband began to field phone calls and questions and inquiries in the lobby after church. The situation became very uncomfortable. And it also became very clear that this person's action had created real confusion and debate among people in the church community.

It was hard to know what to do. Ultimately, my friend decided to first privately confront the person who was spreading this incorrect information. That approach comes from the words of Jesus in Matthew 18:15: "If your fellow believer sins against you, you must go to that one privately and attempt to resolve the matter. If he responds, your relationship is restored" (TPT). To my friend, it seemed that this person's actions qualified as sinning against her, since the woman was telling a story that wasn't the truth. Had it been a difference of opinion or preference, my friend might have just left it alone. But this situation seemed more serious than that because it was causing repercussions beyond my friend and this person.

The conversation did not go well. Initially, my friend asked this person what she had been saying. Her hope was that the comment had been taken out of context. But, in fact, this person stood by what she had been saying and went even further, stating that my friend and her husband were being materialistic and selfish. It shocked my friend; this was not what she had expected. She decided that she didn't need to say anything more to this person unless there could be another person or two there to create accountability, not just for the person spreading the rumors, but also for my friend so that she could try to avoid the temptation to go nuclear.

That's also the next step Jesus gave when it comes to ending relational procrastination and dealing with difficult interpersonal challenges. Continuing in Matthew 18:16, he said, "But if his heart is closed to you, then go to him again, taking one or two others with you. You'll be fulfilling what the Scripture teaches when it says, 'Every word may be verified by the testimony of two or three witnesses'" (TPT). So my friend enlisted the help of a trusted mentor, someone both my friend and the person making these claims respected. But that didn't go well either.

My friend will tell you that as much as she was trying to handle all this in a godly way, she struggled. It was painful for someone to come against her husband's character and erode the reputation of her family. There were moments in these two confrontational encounters that my friend found her temper getting really hot. There are things she could have expressed in a more mature way. The aspects that stung the most personally were probably the things that, long term, she could have ignored.

But what couldn't be ignored was the impact the conflict could have had on their faith community. It could have been polarizing. It could have pulled people onto sides. For that reason, my friend decided to pull into the light what had been in the dark.

It falls in line with what Paul told Titus about how to handle conflicts like this at the church at Crete. Paul wrote to Titus and said, "Warn a divisive person once, and then warn them a second time. After that, have nothing to do with them" (Titus 3:10). The issue was personal, but it also had public ramifications, and that was the reason my friend felt she had to act.

That leads me to a little something Solomon wrote: "[There is] a time to be silent and a time to speak" (Eccl. 3:7). I'm learning the difference.

I think this is a great guide for how to determine what we need to speak up about and what we simply need to let love cover. Every small irritant, every difference of opinion, every preference does not have to be something we call out. We don't have to have a dog in every fight. I love the way the Passion Translation renders Proverbs 17:27–28:

> Can you bridle your tongue when your heart is under
>      pressure?
> That's how you show that you are wise.
> An understanding heart keeps you cool, calm, and collected,
> no matter what you're facing.
> When even a fool bites his tongue
> he's considered wise.
> So shut your mouth when you are provoked—
> it will make you look smart.

There are times when the mute button is your best approach. That means removing yourself from the situation, choosing not to comment, and giving yourself a little space. But sometimes, a more dramatic protocol is necessary. If someone has crossed the line, is a danger to others, is compromising the unity of a faith community, or is slandering or extorting others, it's time to unfollow that person.

You might think that seems harsh, but that's what Jesus calls us to do when someone's behavior has moved beyond a certain point.

Let's pick back up in Matthew 18. Look at what Jesus said about a person who has sinned against you, and you've first tried talking privately with that person and then brought a couple other people along to help. If none of that has worked, it comes down to this: "If they still refuse to listen, tell it to the church; and if they refuse to listen even to the church, treat them as you would a pagan or a tax collector" (Matt. 18:17). I don't claim that it's easy to find the courage to speak up and turn the lights on in the dark. It's hard. It takes a lot of wisdom. But here's where one of the promises of God is key as you discern what to simply mute and what to unfollow by taking decisive action. James, the brother of Jesus, wrote this: "If any of you lacks wisdom, you should ask God, who gives generously to all without finding fault, and it will be given to you" (James 1:5). Wisdom in these situations is ours for the asking.

## JUDGING OR JUDICIOUS?

There were many reasons for the procrastination and avoidance I used in various situations. Threats from my childhood abuser. Shame. Fear. But there is another reason we use today in our faith culture: being blamed for "judging" someone. If we aren't careful how we define the word *judge*, it can keep us from speaking up when we should.

Look, I would rather err on the side of grace than call someone out in a way that ultimately means I'm judging that person. But for followers of Christ, making righteousness our goal and encouraging others on to righteousness isn't judging. It's judicious.

*Judicious* sounds a lot like *judging*, but it's different. It means that you've used wisdom and good judgment in a situation. It doesn't mean "judging" in the sense that you are setting the code for what is right and what is wrong. The sexual abuser who stole my childhood? I'm not judging him when I speak about what happened with him and I seek to protect others; I'm being judicious. When you get a phone call from a friend asking about that person you know gossiped about them? You're not judging when you speak the truth about what you experienced. You're being judicious.

While I myself have experienced the judgmental environment that church folks sometimes slather on, I don't want to lose the God-given privilege of speaking up when something isn't right. Make sure when you're faced with a situation in which you could speak up or remain silent that you think through the options: Would speaking up be judgmental? Or would it be judicious? A judicious heart, empowered by the Holy Spirit, can make the right call.

## AND THIS . . .

While working on this chapter, I started looking at places in the Word of God where people avoided dealing with certain situations, where they procrastinated in speaking up and taking action. There are several different examples of this, but there was one that kept coming back to me.

The Good Samaritan.

Jesus told stories to his followers to help them understand and remember kingdom concepts. We call these stories *parables* because they are composed of one set of circumstances that carry a deeper meaning alongside situations in our lives. Parables apply to our experiences.

In the parable of the good Samaritan, which is found in Luke 10, a man was traveling from Jerusalem to Jericho when he was jumped by bandits, beaten, and left for dead by the side of the road. First, a priest encountered the injured man, and then a Levite, another religious leader. Both of these men avoided helping the victim by seemingly being too busy or expecting someone else to help him. They had their excuses, but they avoided taking care of the injured person. Ultimately, it was a Samaritan who helped him. The religious leaders in Jesus' day hated the Samaritan people because they didn't exactly follow the theology of the Jews. But Jesus showed that those willing to help the wounded act with more righteousness than the religious who avoid those in need.

Here's my thought: I've been the beaten traveler. I've been busted up on this journey of life. At the same time, I've also been the religious person, passing my wounded self by, too busy with other things or too worried about the consequences of stopping and getting myself the help I need. I've avoided dealing with situations that left me by the side of the road, robbed of innocence and hope. I've been in both roles at the same time.

Maybe that's you too. Where have you avoided speaking up when you needed to, or dealing with something head on, or making a necessary change? Can I suggest that when we do that, we're not only the victim on the side of the road, but we're also the person passing by? We have the Holy Spirit in us that longs to comfort and counsel and infuse us with courage to face evil head on.

I want to remember the righteousness of the Samaritan in Jesus' parable. I want to remember that sometimes the person on the side of the road is me, and using my voice is one way to get me on down the road to the inn where I can find the care I need, just like the inn the Good Samaritan took the injured traveler to.

It's time to face what has haunted you. It's time to quit making a big deal out of little things and deal with the big thing that's been the root of the problem all along. Root canals aren't fun, but they are necessary to clean out and heal what has been hidden. Ending toxic relationships and calling them out for what they are is scary. Finding your voice when you've been on mute for so long is hard. But this is the way we exit the Trap of Avoidance. This is how we end procrastinating in the big things. We speak up. And our words, guided by the Holy Spirit, bring cleansing, truth, healing, and safety to a new day.

## BEFORE WE MOVE ON

1. What have you not spoken up about that needs to be brought into the light?
2. What has kept you silent?
3. What would it mean to act as the Good Samaritan toward yourself?
4. What has avoidance cost you?
5. What would leaving the Trap of Avoidance do for your future?

*nine*

# PRACTICE THE BEST REVENGE

FROM WHAT I CAN TELL, GEORGE HERBERT WAS SORT of the Tom Hanks of the seventeenth century. He was one of those guys who seemed to have a talent for whatever he decided to pursue. He was born into a family of ten kids in England. Early in his life, he thought he wanted to be a pastor. After his time at college, where he earned his bachelor's and master's degrees by the time he was twenty-three, he became what we would think of today as the face of the brand for his university, representing Cambridge as a public speaker. He was so good that he caught the eye of King James I—yeah, that King James. He also became a member of Parliament. In his spare time, he became a pastor and writer.

So, you know, an underachiever.

In spite of chronic bad health, Herbert wrote a wealth of poems and literature and music, in addition to managing his academic career and his position in Parliament. Ever hear the phrase "His bark is worse than his bite?" It's in a collection of English sayings he compiled called *Outlandish Proverbs*. Among that collection of insightful and witty maxims sits number 524:

Living well is the best revenge.[1]

Which, at the end of the day, sounds a whole lot like these words from Jesus: "The thief comes only to steal and kill and destroy; I have come that they may have life, and have it to the full" (John 10:10).

There's something about living in the middle of unresolved hurt that can make you put your life on pause. You can almost feel as if you're betraying your cause if you laugh, have a beautiful meal with your family, experience a time of joyful worship, or just have a restful night of sleep. It's taken me a long time to figure this out, and I want to make sure you get it: when you don't practice "the best revenge," you allow the hurt to rob you all over again.

You can wait for God to take action *and* move forward in your life. You can hold a standard of righteousness *and* have a good laugh. In the midst of hurt, in the midst of wounds, in the midst of waiting on God as your Defender, you can take action. You can engage in the best of God's practices for fully living.

Your action plan includes these items for living well: active rest, time with family, gratitude, worship, counsel, and blessing. Let's spend some time on each of these.

## ACTIVE REST

Living in the wake of being wronged is exhausting. It's a bone-deep, marrow-crushing kind of tired, am I right? In the first moments of experiencing someone gossiping about me, or crossing a line, or taking from me, there's that initial adrenaline rush. Anger has its own kind of hum, and for the first little bit following a hurt, I'm revved up, looking for ways to make things right, making the necessary phone calls, reviewing and replaying the conversation in my head.

But then comes the aftermath.

Do you know what I'm talking about? It's that place where the adrenaline subsides, your brain chemistry and spirit crash, and you find yourself drained and deflated.

In the past, I would allow being drained and deflated to turn into what I thought was rest, but it really wasn't. I'd find myself sleepy in the middle of the day, napping to get away from the yucky feelings left behind in hurt's wake. I'd put off certain chores and activities because my soul felt too tender to venture out. I'd think I was taking care of myself, giving myself some "me time," but all too often, it would simply devolve into a numbing fatigue.

King David felt this sense of the sapped soul too. He wrote these words in Psalm 69, one of the imprecatory psalms we talked about earlier that were specifically written about wrongs he had faced, his feelings about those times, and his cry to God for justice:

> Save me, O God,
>> for the waters have come up to my neck.
> I sink in the miry depths,
>> where there is no foothold.
> I have come into the deep waters;
>> the floods engulf me.
> I am worn out calling for help;
>> my throat is parched.
> My eyes fail,
>> looking for my God.
> Those who hate me without reason
>> outnumber the hairs of my head;
> many are my enemies without cause,
>> those who seek to destroy me. (vv. 1–4)

Look at the strong words David used to express how he felt in the midst of waiting for God's deliverance. They all have a physical connection to what he was feeling emotionally. He felt as though he was drowning: "I sink in the miry depths." He was tired: "I am worn out." He was feeling a sore throat coming on: "My throat is parched." Everything was looking dim: "My eyes fail."

That's why I think active rest is important for body and soul.

We know as followers of God how important Sabbath is. Sabbath is the practice of setting aside a lot of our daily activities and taking time to be with God and rest. Active rest can be like that as we wait to see how God will step in as our Defender.

Going on long walks. Eating things that nourish and strengthen your body. Taking bubble baths. Cleaning out that closet that makes you itch. These are examples of things that give you quiet time without diving into a blinds-drawn, huddle-under-the-covers-for-days situation.

## TIME WITH FAMILY

When I'm dealing with a wrong, whether someone is coming against me or there's a business situation in which someone isn't being ethical, I tend to isolate myself. It's not easy for me to compartmentalize my pain, so I remove myself as a way to keep it from sloshing onto my family.

But when I do that, as rightly motivated as I am, I rob myself, my husband, and my kids of my presence. I'll do it with my extended family as well, and it's not helpful. It ends up making me feel more alone, and it costs me precious time with the people I love most.

Planning and enjoying that big birthday bash for your aunt isn't going to get you any closer to winning the business deal that's gone south. But it will give you something else to think about. It will give your focus a new place to live, and it will bless one of your family members. Don't wander off from family dinners. Don't miss movie night with your kids. Time with your family can help keep you grounded and remind you of what is most important.

There's a Bible verse I think about in relation to this. Paul wrote two letters to Timothy that we know of, when Timothy was pastoring the church in Ephesus. When it came to family dynamics, Paul wanted Timothy to make sure the church knew this: "Anyone who does not provide for their relatives, and especially for their own household, has denied the faith and is worse than an unbeliever" (1 Tim. 5:8). Now Paul was definitely speaking about providing for one's family financially. Some people in the young church at Ephesus apparently thought the church should provide some kind of financial assistance for them, and Paul wanted to set the record straight that those who could work should—that is part of our obedience in following Jesus. It seems to me that providing for our family is, yes, partly financial. But it's also emotional—by being together, showing up, being present for each other. We fully provide for each other by meeting financial, emotional, and companionship needs.

While I never intend to neglect my family when I'm hurting, I can if I'm not careful. You can too. Stay alert. Stay aware. Schedule time to be with your family, your people. Commit to making it something other than rehashing that hurtful situation you're dealing with. Celebrate your people, have the family game night, have that dance party in the kitchen while you clean up after dinner. Show up for your family and let God babysit the wrongs you're processing.

# GRATITUDE

I know, I know. We can create really trite memes about how counting our blessings makes us realize everything we do have. And there's truth in that. But there is also truth in how much an inequity against us can cost. Someone may have wrongfully taken money from you. Maybe your ex-husband was able to afford a better lawyer, and now he's got more custody of the kids than you do—and he's the one who had the affair! It's hard to mine for things to be grateful for in a dark cave of despair.

But here's the way I look at it: the most powerful kind of gratitude isn't circumstantial. Oh, I usually practice a circumstantial gratitude. Often in my quiet time when I'm jotting down what I am grateful for, I can veer all too easily into naming the pretty weather and the great new restaurant Abel and I went to for date night the previous evening. I should be grateful for those things, but that's circumstantial gratitude.

See, the kind of gratitude that sustains us, even through wrongs and unfair situations, is what I call *uncircumstantial gratitude*. Here's what I mean: I want to live in a state of gratitude whatever my situation may be. Outside of anything else, beyond anything I might consider a blessing in my life, I want to live in gratitude as someone who is called a child of God because of the salvation he has given me, with an identity and a future that no human can take away.

I didn't say I was there yet. I know I have a long way to go. I've got a great mentor in the apostle Paul. He said,

I have learned how to be content with whatever I have. I know how to live on almost nothing or with everything. I have learned the secret of living in every situation, whether it is with a full stomach or empty, with plenty or little. For I can do everything through Christ, who gives me strength. (Phil. 4:11–13 NLT)

I find it very interesting that Paul's words "For I can do everything through Christ, who gives me strength" follow a whole list of situations, all the circumstances he found himself in, that competed for his outlook. Hungry or full, flush with cash or broke, Paul found that he could handle any of it with power, because Jesus gave him the strength to do it. Paul lived in a state of *uncircumstantial gratitude*, and in so doing, he lived the best revenge against his enemies because he was living well.

So, yes, keep a list of the things you are grateful for, even in the midst of unjust losses. Those markers are helpful when life seems overwhelming and biased. And extend that gratitude even further to other areas of your life and watch those areas flourish.

## WORSHIP

Can I be honest? Sometimes when something has come against me that is really hurting my heart, I kind of want to avoid praise and worship music. Now I know that doesn't make sense, since I love God with all my heart and soul. Let me explain.

When I worship, whether by myself or at a Sunday church service, I immediately feel better. Everything brightens. Hope floods my heart. Right now, I listen on repeat to the song "Surrounded (Fight My Battles)" by UPPERROOM.

And let's not miss the power of worshiping with others. Hearing the unity of all those voices, all of us praising God together and believing him for big things, is one of the most powerful experiences I know to remind me that I'm not alone. I'm part of a family of God's children, and God's Word tells us that our prayers and our praise are powerful.

So why wouldn't I run straight to worshiping when times are hard? Great question. Here's what I think I've figured out—and maybe this is true for you too: sometimes I want to soak in the sad awhile, and I know if I get my worship on, I'm going to leave that soaking a lot earlier. Sometimes it feels good to feel bad.

Please tell me I'm not the only one.

I want to challenge you with this: when those feelings are swirling, put on that praise music.

Listen, all great movies have great soundtracks, right? Part of what makes a story powerful is the music it is set to. Make a soundtrack for your life. Include songs about the greatness of God, how God defends you and lifts you up, how he is the Father who loves his children. Then play it on repeat. Listen to it on your commute. Put on your headphones and listen to it while you work around the house. Play it over the speakers in your home so that you're allowing those life-giving words to flow over your family as well. Music isn't the only means of worship, but it is such a powerful one. Music is what brought down the walls of the enemy at Jericho (Joshua 6). The worshipers went out in front of the army in 2 Chronicles 20 to pave the way for victory. Worship brings glory to God and life to my heart, and it's a weapon against the schemes of the Enemy.

## COUNSEL

All throughout Scripture, I see people who actively sought and employed and engaged trusted counselors to help them sort through their challenges. Moses had his father-in-law, Jethro, who helped him deal with the stress of overseeing the nation of Israel and gave him practical advice that enabled Moses to walk in a more capable and healthy way in his calling. Exodus 18 gives the full account of Moses and Jethro's counseling session.

Three things in the passage really stand out to me. The first is this powerful question Jethro asked Moses: "What are you really accomplishing here?" (Ex. 18:14 NLT).

Sister, please hear me: you've got to have people in your life who are brave enough and wise enough to ask you this question. There are times when I have let my feelings and situations become everything I'm living for. And I'm thankful for the wise Christian therapists in my life who have asked me what Jethro did: *How is this emotion serving you? How is this focus on wanting vengeance making your life better? How are you accomplishing the goal of growing closer to God through all of this?*

Sometimes, as it was in Moses' life, you may have a family member who can be that person for you. But often, someone outside the situation, someone who is skilled and trained in helping people through trauma, is the person you need to engage. Even though Jethro was Moses' father-in-law, he and Moses didn't live in close proximity once Moses began leading the Israelites. Jethro came from out of town to visit Moses when they had the counseling session recorded in Exodus 18. It's important to note that this degree of separation gave Jethro insight and a better view of how Moses was really doing.

"You're going to wear yourself out," Jethro told Moses (Ex. 18:18 NLT). After he challenged Moses to identify why he was living the way he was, subjecting himself to frustration and overwhelming circumstances, Jethro was able to help Moses see how the situation was robbing him of living abundantly.

"Now listen to me, and let me give you a word of advice, and may God be with you," Jethro said next (Ex. 18:19 NLT). And here's what's important: for counsel to work, we have to take it. We have to implement it. We have to receive it. It doesn't do us any good to take the time to go to a counselor or meet with a trusted mentor if all we're going to do is argue why their suggested approach can't possibly work. I know, I know. Your situation is unique. Your hurt and the justice you want to see are original. But there are powerful precepts that can apply to whatever you are facing. The willingness and humbleness to allow a trusted person to speak into that situation will bring great value as you wait upon God as your Defender.

# BLESSING

When I was in late middle school and early high school, in addition to being obese and wearing secondhand-store clothes, I began to develop the strangest rash. Patches of angry red skin stamped up my arms. That rash itched like crazy, and I couldn't help but scratch it, which made it even angrier and grossly weepy besides. The worse it looked, the more self-conscious I was about it. I was already dressing in huge T-shirts and hiding my large figure under loose layers of clothing. But as this weird rash got worse and worse, I started wearing sweaters all the time to cover it up. Now, for a kid living in Southern California, this sweater camouflage wasn't always the most comfortable or practical. When temperatures hit the midnineties, it was downright miserable to be both itchy and hot.

One particularly hot day, I took off my sweater to try to get some relief, which left me wearing only an oversize, short-sleeve T-shirt. I thought my arms didn't look too bad that day, and I was weighing being hot, with my face beet red, against being a little more comfortable but with my rashy arms exposed. I figured taking off my sweater while I was in the lunch line would be the easiest. I could twist my forearms up while I carried my lunch tray, and then, once I was sitting down, I could keep my left arm hidden under the cafeteria table, quickly move my right hand to take a bite of food, and then tuck that arm back under the table too. *Good plan*, I congratulated myself.

The plan went sour pretty fast.

Some girls began making fun of the rash on my arms. It started out subtly but escalated pretty quickly into pointing at me and calling me out.

I don't know that I've ever felt so naked.

The sweater went back on and stayed there.

But there was one place I couldn't hide: the volleyball court. I was part of the volleyball team, and I loved to play. I loved the strategy. I loved how you have to stay mentally in the game; you've got to keep your eye not just on where the ball currently is but on where it could be heading. My busy brain, with its constant barrage of thoughts and worries and self-condemnation, would get much quieter when I was on the volleyball court, tracking the ball and the net and the other players. But the sport required that all of us wear the same practice and game uniforms. The tank-top-style uniform was not a friend to a self-conscious teenage girl with a weird rash on her arms.

There was a girl on my team I admired so much. She was beautiful and petite and an absolute powerhouse on the court. She was one of those athletes who combined a great work ethic with a natural athleticism. Compared to the taller frames of the other players, she looked tiny, and I'm sure opposing teams didn't think she looked threatening at all. But once the first serve went over the net, she weaponized. She just knew where the ball was headed. Her vertical jump was ridiculous, and she could spike the ball back into our opponents' court with seismic force. I looked up to her so much, for her skill and her drive. We hadn't become close friends in the previous season, but I was hoping to get to know her better.

When we gathered for the new volleyball season, I was heavier than I had ever been, and my rash was particularly bad. I hadn't yet purchased the knee pads our team required, and last season the girls, laughing, had said they'd buy me some since my parents couldn't afford them. None of that affected my volleyball skill, but I headed into the first practice feeling really self-conscious. And it was hot. There was no way I could get away with wearing my trusty sweater on that court; I would have collapsed of heatstroke. So into the team uniform sleeveless tank top I went, along with the practice shorts. All the skin issues and unhealthy weight gain were there for my teammates to see.

I headed out to the team huddle for warm-ups. And this girl, this athlete I admired, looked at me with disgust in her eyes. "Rosie," she said, distaste peppering her tone, "how could you let this happen to you?" She took a step back, taking in all of me and shaking her head. There she stood, in all of her petite, beautiful, muscled, sculpted glory, judgment over both the expanse and condition of my skin stamped on her pretty face.

I didn't know it was possible for me to feel worse about myself until that moment. But when someone you look up to and admire shows nothing but disappointment and disgust in you, it drops you even further.

Those two experiences—the lunch-line ridicule and the volleyball-court shaming—remained seared on my heart for years. For a long while, as I continued on a self-destructive path of overeating, undereating, and partying, those two moments played over and over in my head. Those girls' voices in my head often overpowered my own. I know sometimes we want to laugh about or underestimate the influence of a mean-girl moment, but it's a dangerous thing, and the effects can last for a very long time.

Fast-forward several years. God had brought a lot of healing to my life. He had seen me through overcoming my self-destructive eating habits, leading to my losing one hundred pounds. The rash on my arms that had plagued me for years had cleared up. I was definitely a late bloomer, but it finally happened. I was comfortable in my own skin and enjoyed dressing up and playing with different makeup looks.

And then this happened.

I actually ran into those girls—one girl I had felt was a friend who made fun of me at lunch, and my volleyball teammate who had publicly commented on my physical appearance. Here's the deal: in the years that had passed since school days, neither of them had aged well. They were both fighting extra weight and physical changes.

I was tempted. I was. There was a part of my heart that felt so validated, so victorious. Even though I wanted to think that I had forgiven much of the hurt in my past, there was something about seeing both of those women in their current conditions that made me recognize a grudge was still there in my heart. I felt a flash of smugness sweep across my spirit. I felt a smirk tug at my inner dialogue. It almost seemed as though I was getting justice for all the mean things they had said. Everything they had made fun of in me was an issue they were dealing with. All kinds of things I could say to them came spilling into my mind. I could have "told them their truth," which is a Latino saying meaning to clap back at someone.

I didn't. God has shown me time and time again that even when people have been mean to me, God loves them too. He doesn't want me to be mean to them. He's going to deal with them.

That's when God showed me another beautiful lesson.

Part of living well as the best form of revenge is understanding that what you say and do can come back to you. God was letting me see vindication for what they had done, but he was also teaching me something very important: our words matter.

I felt him saying to me, *With your tongue, you bless or you curse. When someone curses you, I work on your behalf. They teased you about your physical condition, but you chose to become disciplined about taking care of your body, and I blessed it. They teased you about being poor, but you chose to work hard, and I blessed it.*

See, sometimes the best revenge God can give you is to bless your life. He doesn't even have to do anything to the other people. He just lets them eat their words.

We say that, don't we, when someone has to walk back what they said? That family member who told you that you would never amount to anything, and now God has opened up a wonderful door of opportunity for you—and they have to eat their words.

I was curious as to where this saying came from. There are all kinds of variations of this phrase in English: *eat crow, eat your heart out, eat humble pie, eat dirt, eat your hat.* But all those variations mean the same thing: what we put out there in what we say can come back to bite us. As I did a little internet search on just where these phrases originated, I discovered it was John Calvin who first put the phrase *eat one's words* out there. John Calvin was the fiery French-born lawyer and minister who was a main figure in the Reformation of the 1500s. He was controversial and passionate, and you may be familiar with his legacy today, since those who adhere to his view of Christianity are called Calvinists. The saying about eating one's words comes from a religious tract he wrote about Psalm 62.[2] And it's in this psalm that we find these incredible words:

> One thing God has spoken,
>     two things I have heard:
> "Power belongs to you, God,
>     and with you, Lord, is unfailing love";
> and, "You reward everyone
>     according to what they have done." (vv. 11–12)

In his tract, Calvin wanted to make it clear that what God speaks is true and complete. In the same Bible where God speaks of his power and his unfailing love is also the word he gives about rewarding people according to what they have done. God doesn't have to eat his words, because he never goes back on them. When we bless others, when we forgive, when we let God be our Defender, it comes back to bless us. We don't have to taste the bitter mouthful of reprisal.

For a long while, I spoke over myself the messages the mean girls had spoken. I repeated over the soft ground of my raw heart the same hurtful words they had said: *I'm fat. I'm so weird with this gross rash. My family can't afford anything.*

But in his patience, God led me to start speaking new messages over my life and stop cursing myself. He taught me that I could change the eating patterns that were compromising my health by declaring his Word: *God has given me a spirit of "power, love and self-discipline"* (2 Tim. 1:7). He helped me break free from a not-enough mindset and claim his provision: *God supplies all my needs (and sometimes my wants!)* (Phil. 4:19). He showed me how to speak and live abundantly instead of declaring more hurt over my life.

Grab hold of these verses:

"Whoever would love life
　　and see good days
　must keep their tongue from evil
　　and their lips from deceitful speech." (1 Peter 3:10)

"What goes into someone's mouth does not defile them, but what comes out of their mouth, that is what defiles them." (Matt. 15:11)

When it comes to practicing the best revenge of living well, declare it.

I don't want to forget to tell you this: Remember how those girls made fun of my appearance and the condition of my skin? Today, I receive incredible gifts of various lotions and potions all the time because of my work in the beauty industry. It's this lovely little reminder that God saw my tears all those years ago and now, to this day, reminds me that he is for me, he sees me, and he loves me.

Now when people make fun of me, I just get ready to see God move in favor in my life. However he chooses to deal with those people, I've learned there is great blessing in letting God keep that his business between him and them. What I look forward to now is seeing how he's going to bring me good. Sometimes in the form of lots of fun skin creams. Sometimes in peace. Sometimes in letting me have a peek at how the story turns out.

Proverbs 25:21–22 says,

　If your enemy is hungry, give him food to eat;
　　if he is thirsty, give him water to drink.
　In doing this, you will heap burning coals on his head,
　　and the LORD will reward you.

Yep. That's right. You continue to practice the rhythms of active rest, time with family, gratitude, and worship. Seek out godly counsel. Be intentional about what you declare out of your mouth. Speak blessing. Refuse to speak hurt to those who have hurt you. Respond in the opposite way to the one who has wounded you. It will bring life. It will bring reward—and God's reward and favor over your life are the ultimate revenge. Live well.

## BEFORE WE MOVE ON

1. How are you intentionally taking care of yourself as you navigate the hurt you have experienced?

2. Where have you been at risk of allowing the hurt you suffered to rob you of more joy? Has It stood in the way of friendships and family relationships?

3. What small step can you take today to reclaim some of the abundance Jesus died to give you?

*ten*

# THE ULTIMATE DEFENDER

WE'VE TRAVELED THROUGH SOME WILD PLACES TO get here, but this is where we experience what it means for God to be our Defender. We've worked through the places where it's easy to get stuck. We've traversed the places where we could justify staying. Now, having processed our agendas and faced some things that perhaps we haven't faced before, we're ready to see God's glory as Defender.

To be clear, there are times when God shows up as Defender, and it's epic. It's something out of a movie, with the bad guys getting their due, with shock and awe, with a clear demonstration of what looks and feels and sounds like justice—like when an evil queen plummets to her death.

Of all the "baddies" in the Bible, Jezebel ranks right up there as one of the worst. She arranged for the murders of many priests and insisted her people bow down to idols. She made threats, intimidated people, and used her power and position to manipulate and kill with abandon. And after all that mayhem, she met a satisfying end. A new king, Jehu, was anointed to lead Israel, and he began to root out the evil influences that had turned the heart of the people away from God. One day he arrived at the house where Jezebel was staying and called up to her window.

Second Kings 9:30–35 says,

> Then Jehu went to Jezreel. When Jezebel heard about it, she put on eye makeup, arranged her hair and looked out of a window.

165

As Jehu entered the gate, she asked, "Have you come in peace, you Zimri, you murderer of your master?"

He looked up at the window and called out, "Who is on my side? Who?" Two or three eunuchs looked down at him. "Throw her down!" Jehu said. So they threw her down, and some of her blood spattered the wall and the horses as they trampled her underfoot.

Jehu went in and ate and drank. "Take care of that cursed woman," he said, "and bury her, for she was a king's daughter." But when they went out to bury her, they found nothing except her skull, her feet and her hands.

The queen's own servants betrayed her. Scripture later reveals that dogs tore at her remains. It's bloody, it's graphic, and it seems like a just outcome for someone who had led such a bloody, graphic life.

But you and I have been hanging out in this world long enough to know that endings to such stories don't always finish on such a clear note.

To invite God to be our Defender, there are truths we must accept. Some of them won't be easy to embrace. Some of them won't initially satisfy our desire for payback in the way we envision. Yet God's ways will always be for our ultimate good.

When he is our Defender . . .

## GOD WILL DEFEND US HIS WAY

I like the phrase *the punishment should fit the crime*. It's a cornerstone of many legal systems in nations across the world. Societies have determined that if someone commits *this*, the price that must be paid is *that*. The concept comes from an ancient Latin phrase *Culpae poena par esto*, which describes how we evaluate the severity of various wrongs and choose to enforce the punishment for those wrongs.

I have my own mental list of *culpae poena par esto*. If people unfairly gossip about me, I have an opinion about how they should pay. If someone hurts someone I love, I have a penalty in mind that I think fits what that person has done. And because I have my own sense of what punishment fits what crime, I have a very specific expectation of what God should do to show himself as my Defender in how he deals with those who have wronged me.

But God isn't just the upholder of righteousness and justice; he is righteousness itself. And he is the Judge, which means he gets to make the rules.

In a courtroom, the judge hears both sides of a case. American legal-drama thrillers and movies usually portray a trial by jury. It's one of the tenets of the American legal system that the accused have the right to have their cases heard in front of a group of peers, and that jury then renders a judgment.

But there's another type of trial that doesn't always get the same kind of cinema play: a bench trial. In a bench trial, the judge not only hears the case but also hands down what is known as his or her "finding," which is just another way of saying "verdict."

I've made the mistake before, and maybe you have too, of thinking of God as presiding over a jury trial. I want to be the prosecutor, who presents to him the evidence of how someone has wronged me. I also want to be a jury member, who gets to decide the verdict and has a say in making the punishment fit the crime.

But from what I can tell from Scripture, God holds only bench trials. He isn't going to allow a pack of well-intentioned and yet agenda-driven humans dictate the outcome of the cases set before him. He hears us when we tell him of the hurts and wrongs we experience. It matters deeply to him. But when God is our Defender, it also means he is the Judge over the case. And his version of *culpae poena par esto* may be very different from yours and mine.

He's the God who welcomed into paradise the criminal who hung on the cross next to Jesus, a man guilty of his crimes who had no chance to make things right. In that heavenly bench trial, God gave that criminal grace (Luke 23:32–43). And he's the God who struck down two early followers of the church, Ananias and Sapphira, for lying about how much profit from a land sale they had actually given to the church (Acts 5).

Now, I gotta be honest. God seemed to go a little easy on the crucified criminal. And he seemed to go a little Rambo on the fibbing real-estate agents. Traditionally, when we talk about the criminal on the cross, we usually refer to him as a thief, which sounds like someone who was pick-pocketing or shoplifting. But the Greek word used to describe the men who hung on either side of Jesus at the execution was *kakourgos*. That word implies that their crimes were evil. So it's possible that God made a verdict for the criminal on the cross that wouldn't satisfy our sense of punishment. If we knew the specifics of this man's crimes, we might even say that, as far as eternity is concerned, he got away with it.

And when I look at the case of Ananias and Sapphira in Acts 5, immediate death for shorting the collection plate seems a little, um, wow.

But this is the reality of God as our Defender. He gets to decide what punishment fits which crime—and he has his reasons. To call on God as your Defender is to release your idea of the appropriate penalty and lean into how he is going to deal with it.

# GOD WILL DEFEND US IN HIS TIME

I'm all about swift justice. I studied criminology in college and later moved on to law school. I always felt a thrill when I read about a case in which the evidence was quickly gathered, the suspect promptly apprehended, the jury speedily seated, and the verdict briskly rendered. It made our justice system seem efficient and trustworthy, and it satisfied my need to see things wrapped up in a manner that seemed fair.

Sometimes God's defense of us is swift. Sometimes it is not, according to our perspective. It doesn't mean he isn't working behind the scenes to vindicate us in ways we can't yet see.

It was years before the person who abused me as a child was ultimately brought to justice. He was a fugitive for nine years, trying to avoid arrest. But when it did happen, it was swift. It was decisive. By the time the case went to court in 2007, it had been eighteen years since he first abused me. By that time, laws and jail time in child sexual-abuse cases had become more severe. Penalties were harsher.[1] And I was at a place in my life where I was able to testify in a much more powerful way than I would have been able to years earlier.

Does any of that explain why it took so long? Maybe. Maybe not. I don't know that it will ever make sense to me in this life.

David wrote a psalm about the challenge of resting in God's timing as your Defender. Some theologians think that Psalm 13 was written as David agonized over the betrayal he experienced from his son Absalom. Absalom took over his father's kingdom in a revolt, and he even slept with his father's concubines in public as an ultimate sign of disrespect. But it wasn't just the politics and sexual escapades of Absalom that were hurtful. David's very life was in danger from his son, and David and a handful of loyal friends had to hide from Absalom and his army. Other theologians say it isn't possible to pinpoint the time in David's life when he wrote Psalm 13, but one thing is clear: David was struggling with God's timeline in coming to his defense.

> How long, LORD? Will you forget me forever?
>> How long will you hide your face from me?
> How long must I wrestle with my thoughts
>> and day after day have sorrow in my heart?
>> How long will my enemy triumph over me?
>
> Look on me and answer, LORD my God.
>> Give light to my eyes, or I will sleep in death,
> and my enemy will say, "I have overcome him,"
>> and my foes will rejoice when I fall.
>
> But I trust in your unfailing love;
>> my heart rejoices in your salvation.
> I will sing the LORD's praise,
>> for he has been good to me. (vv. 1–6)

Did you count them? Four times. Four times in just a handful of verses, David asks, "How long?" Those "how longs" highlight the key places I have struggled with God's timing in my own life.

"How long, LORD? Will you forget me forever?"
*Will you forget me forever? Are you going to do something? Can you show me you're here?*

"How long will you hide your face from me?"
*Are you hiding from me, God? Do you even see what is
happening here? Are you listening?*

"How long must I wrestle with my thoughts and day after
day have sorrow in my heart?"
*How long will this situation roll over and over in my heart
and mind?*

"How long will my enemy triumph over me?"
*How long will you allow this person to hurt me, think
they've won, and continue with their battle against me?*

These are all valid questions, questions I believe God under-
stands, since he includes them in his Holy Word. But please know
this: I've wrestled with God over these questions. He is big enough
to take it. And he has shown me something amazing along the
way: the answer to each of those questions above is, *I am here.*

Will you forget me forever?
*I am here.*

Will you hide your face from me?
*I am here.*

How long will I wrestle this?
*I am here.*

How long will my enemy triumph?
*I am here.*

God gave me a clear and specific vision that when I've been in some of the most hurtful situations of my life, he has been there. In the midst of some of the most horrible things that have happened to me, he was cradling me in his lap. Christ covered me with his robe, even though the situation around me was appalling. In that moment, he was already planning my vindication.

This response won't completely answer all the questions of your heart. It won't wrap it all up in a neat bow. But when your heart cries, "How long?"—and it will—hear his mysterious and powerful answer.

*I am here.*

There is a New Testament passage that was written to address the human question of God's timing and the disbelief that he will act. Peter reminded his readers,

> By God's word, the present heaven and earth are designated to be burned. They are being kept until the day ungodly people will be judged and destroyed. Dear friends, don't ignore this fact: One day with the Lord is like a thousand years, and a thousand years are like one day. (2 Peter 3:7–8 NOG)

Peter wasn't the only one to give us insight into what time is like for God. Psalm 90 is attributed to Moses, which means it is one of the earliest psalms written. Moses wrote: "A thousand years in your sight are like a day that has just gone by, or like a watch in the night" (v. 4). That says to me that if I want to embrace the righteousness and justice of God, I must at the same time embrace his timing for my defense, which might look far different from mine.

*I am here.*

# GOD'S MERCY ALSO EXTENDS TO THE ONES WHO WRONGED YOU

I am so thankful for the mercy of God. I need it. I rely on it.

We sometimes talk about grace and mercy as if they are the same or are interchangeable. But I've heard it taught—and I believe it to be true—that grace and mercy are separate and distinct. One of the simpler ways I've heard the difference explained is this: grace is God giving us favor that we don't deserve, while his mercy is withholding punishment that we do deserve.

Believe me, I've done a lot of things for which I absolutely deserved whatever punishment might have come my way. God's mercy has saved me from that punishment on many occasions.

God's amazing, mysterious, necessary mercy is one of the aspects of God that I find most incredible. Daniel 9:9 puts it this way: "The Lord our God is merciful and forgiving, even though we have rebelled against him." When I consider the years I lived in rebellion to his call to righteousness, and the ways I still fail, I see that his mercy is all that has stood between me and my own self-destructiveness. I find this description of our merciful God powerful:

> Who is a God like you,
>> who pardons sin and forgives the transgression
>> of the remnant of his inheritance?
>
> You do not stay angry forever,
>> but delight to show mercy.
>
> You will again have compassion on us;
>> you will tread our sins underfoot
>> and hurl all our iniquities into the depths of the sea.
>> (Mic. 7:18–19)

Loving God's mercifulness also opens up a whole other way of looking at his role as my Defender, because here's what I've always known about him: God is about the business of saving people.

Which means that he is God the merciful Defender.

Think about that. Don't just give that sentence a casual glance. When we really take it in, when we understand that saving people is always the motive of God, it changes the conversation.

The apostle Peter wrote about this important facet of God:

> The Lord isn't slow to do what he promised, as some people think. Rather, he is patient for your sake. He doesn't want to destroy anyone but wants all people to have an opportunity to turn to him and change the way they think and act. (2 Peter 3:9 NOG)

That's our God, the Father who wants everyone to have a chance to change how they are living and turn to him.

Gulp.

We love to love a God of mercy when that mercy is extended to us. We struggle with a God of mercy who extends that mercy to people we feel are in the wrong.

But if I want mercy for myself, then I have to accept that those who have hurt me may also receive the mercy of God. It's not injustice on his part. It's not a minimization of what has happened to me. It's something in keeping with who he is.

The Bible offers a beautiful promise if we are willing to align with our God of justice and mercy. "With the merciful," Scripture says, "You will show Yourself merciful" (2 Sam. 22:26 NKJV). I want to show others the kind of mercy I want to be shown. My itch to experience revenge won't always be gratified, but my need for outlandish mercy will be met.

# WE MAY GET TO SEE GOD DEFEND US

Sometimes we do. Moses got to watch the Red Sea swallow Pharaoh's army. The Israelites got to watch David, as the agent of God's revenge, strike down the potty-mouthed giant Goliath. Gideon got to see God exact a miraculous victory over the Midianites. God may show up in the timing you hoped for and dramatically right the wrong. If that happens for you, I want you to rejoice. I rejoiced when the man who was my abuser received his sentence, because it meant future potential victims were now safe.

But I needed to have the Holy Spirit watch over me so that I didn't gloat. To gloat is to have a sense of "malicious satisfaction, [and] ponder with pleasure something that satisfies an evil passion."[2] For me, that "evil passion" could have been revenge. But God's Word is clear about who we should be and how we should act when we see his justice come against those who have sinned against us. Proverbs 24:17–18 says,

> Do not gloat when your enemy falls;
>     when they stumble, do not let your heart rejoice,
> or the LORD will see and disapprove
>     and turn his wrath away from them.

Don't remove the consequence the Lord may have put in place for you to see by giving into a satisfied sense of revenge. Maintain the justice God has attained on your behalf by rejoicing in his righteousness and faithfulness instead of crowing about the consequences for those who have hurt you. Glorify your God, not your gloat.

# WE MAY NEVER GET TO SEE
# GOD DEFEND US

When I was a kid, I liked knowing when my brothers got in trouble. I really liked knowing exactly what each of their punishments was going to be for what they had done. And I really, really liked knowing that if I got into trouble with one of them, they were going to get the same level of punishment I did.

I made it my business to be in my brothers' business when it came to how my mom and dad disciplined us.

Now my kids do the same thing. They are oh-so-curious as to how long Big Sister got grounded after being sassy. They want to know for exactly how long Brother's electronics have been taken away after he broke a rule. Now I get why it bothered my parents so much when I wanted the lowdown on every correction and disciplinary action they took. It's downright irritating to have my kids asking me all kinds of questions about how I'm handling a situation. As a mom, I don't always think it's my kids' business to know how I am dealing with one of their siblings. Sometimes the consequence needs to be only between the child I am dealing with and me. I think it's right as a parent, and sometimes better for the child I'm correcting, not to have that process be in the broader public eye.

But I've got to admit that I'm all kinds of curious about how God is dealing with some of the people who have wronged me in my life. It's one of the ways I've tried in the past to verify that God is acting as my Defender. When I see a consequence play out in someone's life, it feels like proof that God has come to my defense. Maybe that's what it was.

Or maybe not.

The apostle Peter had a history of wanting to keep tabs on

how Jesus was handling issues with the other disciples. In John 21, Peter and Jesus had a long exchange about their relationship and the level of Peter's devotion to ministry. Jesus revealed what it would cost Peter to shepherd the coming church, and that description was heavy. But check out what Peter wanted to know when Jesus made that disclosure to him:

> "Very truly I tell you, when you were younger you dressed yourself and went where you wanted; but when you are old you will stretch out your hands, and someone else will dress you and lead you where you do not want to go." Jesus said this to indicate the kind of death by which Peter would glorify God. Then he said to him, "Follow me!"
>
> Peter turned and saw that the disciple whom Jesus loved was following them. (This was the one who had leaned back against Jesus at the supper and had said, "Lord, who is going to betray you?") When Peter saw him, he asked, "Lord, what about him?"
>
> Jesus answered, "If I want him to remain alive until I return, what is that to you? You must follow me." Because of this, the rumor spread among the believers that this disciple would not die. But Jesus did not say that he would not die; he only said, "If I want him to remain alive until I return, what is that to you?" (vv. 18–23)

Did you catch it? Peter didn't ask for specifics from Jesus about his death. Peter didn't ask if there was another way or if there was something he could do to both follow Jesus and avoid that kind of outcome. Nope. He wanted to know if the same thing was going to happen to John (the disciple Jesus loved)! Classic.

Each of my kids responds to a different style of correction.

For one of them, a stern talking-to does the trick. For another, it's going to take a bigger response, like taking away favorite privileges. For my third child, his tender heart convicts him far more deeply than anything I come up with. I use different methods of dealing with my kids based on how God has wired them, but I have one objective at the end of the day: I want their hearts to be focused on the right things and on God.

How much more does God want that for his kids? And what does that mean for how God acts as our Defender?

He deals with each of us in a customized way. He may choose to deal with the behavior privately. He will act with the purpose of hopefully bringing us to a place of repentance and salvation.

And you and I may not get to see exactly how he does that. Can you accept those terms?

## GOD MY SAVIOR, GOD MY DEFENDER

Accepting the way God works is sometimes hard for me. It would feel neater and more resolved to clearly see a consequence play out in the life of someone who has wronged me. Sometimes I have seen that consequence play out, but it doesn't seem to go far enough. It doesn't seem like a steep enough price to pay for the pain the person caused.

It's a comfort to me that I'm not alone in feeling that way. Paul wrote about it in a letter to the believers who were living in Rome. He was in Corinth when he wrote this letter around AD 57. Interestingly, he hadn't yet traveled to Rome, but he was aware of what the young church there was experiencing. Nero had become the emperor of Rome just four years earlier. He was only sixteen years old when he took the throne. This is the Nero who would have his own mother murdered. This is the Nero who, ten years into his reign, would ultimately blame Christians for a devastating fire in Rome. This is the Nero who would violently persecute the early church. This is the Nero who would sentence Paul to death near the end of his reign. The believers in Rome were already living under the shadow of a malignant man.

Paul's letter to the Romans addressed so many issues about salvation and God's grace. He spent a lot of time explaining to the new church that God's plan of salvation was extended for everyone, not just the Jews. See, the Jews had been promised a savior, and understandably, they thought that savior would be for them and them alone. But God's plan also included salvation for the Gentiles, those outside of the Jewish faith whom the Jews had long counted if not enemies then at least those who were to be kept at arm's length and regarded with suspicion. The Gentiles hadn't been following God's ways. Why shouldn't they simply get what was coming to them for their generations of unrighteousness? Why wouldn't God's defense of Israel mean serious repercussions against Gentiles? And why would a Jewish savior pay the debt for them?

Paul put pen to paper and, through the inspiration of the Holy Spirit, wrote these incredible words:

What then shall we say? Is God unjust? Not at all! For he says to Moses,

"I will have mercy on whom I have mercy,
and I will have compassion on whom I have
compassion."

It does not, therefore, depend on human desire or effort, but on God's mercy. For Scripture says to Pharaoh: "I raised you up for this very purpose, that I might display my power in you and that my name might be proclaimed in all the earth."

Therefore God has mercy on whom he wants to have mercy. (Rom. 9:14–18)

Sometimes God defends us in just the way we would hope. The abuser goes to jail. The extortionist gets caught. The marriage between the cheating spouse and the girlfriend he left you for fails.

But often, God's defense seems far different from the vindication we were looking for. Our God is the one who made an apostle out of someone who approved of the execution of the first Christian martyr, Stephen. Our God is the one who extended salvation to Nineveh after all their shenanigans, which made the whale-riding prophet Jonah depressed because God didn't follow through with the fireworks and brimstone. Trusting God's *brand* of defense also requires trusting in his *means* of defense, even when they seem invisible or the timing is all off. As Paul wrote in Romans 12:19, "Do not take revenge, my dear friends, but leave room for God's wrath, for it is written: 'It is mine to avenge; I will repay,' says the Lord."

God's methods of defense will never fail us, but they may mystify us. Rest in them anyway. His justice may be something that pays forward to the generation after you. Rest in it anyway. His retribution may turn to mercy in the face of repentance from the one who wronged you. Rest in that mercy. You may see a swift and powerful justice. Rest not in pride but in his providence. God is your ultimate Defender, which means that you will experience that defense in this life or perhaps in the next. But it is there. Beyond your sight, beyond your measure.

It is there, because he says, *I am here.*

## eleven

# TRUE RESTORATION

I HAD ACHIEVED THE ULTIMATE FASHION HACK.

A few months ago, I had been invited to attend a wedding. I wanted something new to wear, something that looked fancy, since this was going to be a more formal wedding. But me being me, I didn't want to spend a whole lot of money. (Your girl Rosie is all about those good bargains.) I also didn't have any extra time to run from store to store, only to find something that was too expensive or didn't come in the right size or in the color I was looking for.

That's when it came to me, a shimmer of bridal boutique brilliance out of the clear blue. I would shop. Oh yes, I would. But I would shop . . . Amazon.

I love me some Amazon. I'm all about that Prime. And I can whiz through Amazon's options quickly without needing to drag myself from dressing room to dressing room across multiple stores. Within just a few short minutes of my fashion brainstorm, I had logged onto my Amazon account, put in a few simple search terms for a fabulous dress, and found just what I was looking for. I had wanted something that was a bit of a risk for me, something midlength in a sheer, lighter color, with beads and pearls sewn into the dress everywhere. And just like that, I found the cutest dress that ticked all the boxes. I quickly tossed my size in the virtual cart, clicked to the checkout, and congratulated myself when my purchase confirmation popped up on the screen.

I was a genius! I was so proud of myself.

And it only cost me seventeen dollars. It was going to take

almost three weeks to arrive, which would mean I'd get it right before the wedding. That was a little concerning to me with my Amazon Prime lifestyle, which ensures that most of my orders arrive in about fourteen minutes. But whatevs.

You already see where this is headed, don't you?

The package finally arrived with just a day to spare before the wedding. I couldn't wait to rip open the shipping box and slip into that adorable dress. I headed to my master bathroom/dressing area and pulled the dress from the box.

Hmm.

Look, I'm no seamstress, so I can't claim technical knowledge on these things, but zippers are supposed to be sewn into a garment in a straight line, correct? Like, zippers aren't supposed to veer off to the left and then bunch for a few inches and then swoop over to the right. I'm pretty sure.

And the material. Oof. It almost felt like some kind of plastic shopping bag, stretched thin and repurposed for clothes. The pearls and beads? Don't get me started. And I don't know what this particular clothing manufacturer was using in terms of sizing, but it wasn't any kind of standard I'm used to. This frock, claiming to be my size, was scaled for one of those creepy "my size" Barbies our daughters all seem to want when they're four years old. Yeah, that kind of sizing. It was quite the fitting session, I can tell you. As in, I was about to throw a fit.

In the middle of my impromptu fitting, my husband came wandering through. You need to know that Abel is a consistently encouraging man, a husband who compliments me frequently and is considerate of the places where my self-esteem and self-image can use a boost. But when he walked through and saw me squished and squeezed into this blingy beige nightmare, he just shook his head.

Yikes. That headshake said it all.

I was trying to stay positive. Surely there was a way to make this work.

I shimmied the dress further up my hips, plastic beads and pearls springing loose and raining down on the marble floor like a miniature hailstorm. I kept shimmying and finally got my arms through the armholes and adjusted the strap over my shoulders. *Better*, I told myself. *This could still work.* I turned from side to side in front of the mirror, my can-do spirit rising.

Abel stood in the background, head still shaking.

I bent over to start gathering up the escaping beads and pearls, telling myself I could bust out the glue gun if I needed to. That's the kind of mania I can experience when something comes with a seventeen dollar price tag.

But as I reached for yet another handful of beads on the floor, the entire back of the dress, held together by that zany zipper highway, gave way.

*Rippppppp!*

At that point, Abel had to physically leave the room to maintain his reputation as an encouraging, sensitive husband and not laugh out loud.

I jumped on the phone with Amazon, demanding an exchange, and they were great, truly. They offered me the options of a refund or having the dress replaced. At that point, I didn't have three more weeks to wait for another version of this dress to come in. Based on my current experience, even if I did have three more weeks available, the odds weren't good that the outcome would be any better.

Ultimately, I had to exchange my idea of getting a one-hundred-dollar look for seventeen dollars for a dress I already had in the back of my closet from a few years ago,

Update: sometimes I still find those little plastic bead-pearl thingies in the nooks and crannies of my bathroom floor.

## WHAT'S THE EXCHANGE RATE?

When we head out on a journey, one of the things we have to consider is the exchange rate for where we're going. Have you ever traveled to another country and gone through the process of exchanging your US dollars for the currency of the country you're visiting? It can be pretty confusing. There's the math involved in determining the equivalent value of the foreign currency to the good old American dollar. When you finally get through exchanging some of your familiar green-and-cream bills for the Technicolor ones other countries use, you'll also find yourself, at every café and market, trying to figure out just how much money in US terms you're spending on each coffee and souvenir. Did I just spend $12.50 on a cup of decaf? Or 12 cents? I can't keep up with it all.

One of the places where it's really confusing to exchange money is in Mexico. I travel there quite a bit for work, and changing money has always been one of the most stressful parts of the trip. A lot of tourists exchange currency at airports in Mexico, and frankly, this is one of the dumbest places to do it. The exchange rates are outrageous, and tourists get taken advantage of over and over because, like me, they're trying to figure out the complicated math in their heads on the fly, and it leaves them even more confused as to what a fair exchange rate is.

But there is a way that the locals exchange their money: they look for an umbrella.

As you drive down certain boulevards, you'll encounter

some gorgeous women, and they'll all be holding umbrellas. If you know, you know. Those women are there to exchange your money, and they'll do it at a fair rate. These umbrella "office" exchanges seem a whole lot shadier (no pun intended) than the slick exchange agencies and kiosks set up at the airport. But the locals know it's the way to go to get the fairest rate.

Whether it's a formal dress with a price tag that turns out to be too good to be true (ahem) or a rip-off exchange rate at the airport, educating ourselves about what things really cost is an important aspect of being equipped to navigate through life well.

When it comes to looking for revenge, justice, or vindication, the exchange rate can feel like the Wild West. We want to exchange the injustice for a certain level of justice. We want to exchange the wrong for a certain degree of punishment for the offender. We want the judgment to be a fair exchange for what happened. But what are the accurate exchange rates? How do we know?

As you and I continue our progress toward fully leaning on God as our Defender, one exchange rate is available that will bring us life and health. But we have to be willing to make the exchange.

## AN I FOR AN I

I happen to like the exchange rate in the Old Testament. You know, the one that called for an eye for an eye? We find it first in Exodus 21:23–25: "If there is serious injury, you are to take life for life, eye for eye, tooth for tooth, hand for hand, foot for foot, burn for burn, wound for wound, bruise for bruise." And it shows up again in Leviticus 24:19–21:

"'Anyone who injures their neighbor is to be injured in the same manner: fracture for fracture, eye for eye, tooth for tooth. The one who has inflicted the injury must suffer the same injury. Whoever kills an animal must make restitution, but whoever kills a human being is to be put to death.'"

This exchange rate makes complete sense to me. If you bust me, I'm gonna bust you.

What's interesting is that this exchange rate was embraced by a lot of different cultures, not just God's chosen people, the Israelites. Another ancient example of this form of justice is in the Code of Hammurabi. It's a whole legal document carved into a piece of polished rock. Archaeologists think it's from about seventeen hundred years before the birth of Jesus. It was discovered in 1901 in the region of ancient Babylon, and if you want to see it today, it's on display at the Louvre in Paris. Chiseled into that stone is the exchange rate of an eye for an eye and a tooth for a tooth. So even cultures that didn't follow God and his precepts certainly embraced this particular exchange rate for dealing with the hurts and injustices that came their way.

Then Jesus showed up. And he turned all of it on its ear. He said,

"You have heard that it was said, 'Eye for eye, and tooth for tooth.' But I tell you, do not resist an evil person. If anyone slaps you on the right cheek, turn to them the other cheek also. And if anyone wants to sue you and take your shirt, hand over your coat as well. If anyone forces you to go one mile, go with them two miles. Give to the one who asks you, and do not turn away from the one who wants to borrow from you." (Matt. 5:38–42)

Huh.

What's going on here? Was Jesus contradicting Scripture? And what's up with this new exchange rate he was promoting? It seems like tourist extortion! How am I supposed to maintain good, healthy boundaries with this kind of exchange rate? How do we keep bad people from doing more bad things if there are no consequences, if there is no follow-up?

We know that Jesus didn't come to contradict Scripture but to fulfill it. The "eye for an eye" passages in the Old Testament were there to guide the nation of Israel as to how to set up their government, how to create a court system. There were passages about witnesses and due process to go along with this Old Testament exchange rate.

But it's easy to see how, over time, people started taking matters into their own hands, creating their own forms of retribution and justifying it with Scripture. What had started out as a way to establish civil peace had become the justification to strike back with equal harshness at someone who had been rude to you. Jesus knew of a better way that would let us experience what the kingdom of heaven is like, as he talked about all through Matthew 5.

Here's what I propose. Let's let go of that "eye for an eye" exchange rate and use this one instead: an "I for an I." Let me show you.

## Exchange "I Am Hurt" for "I Am Healed"

For a long, long time, "hurt" was one of the primary ways I saw myself. If I had to describe myself to someone, I usually led with a list of the things I had experienced at the hands of the sexual abuser who haunted my childhood. Then I would move on to the toxic relationships of my late teens and early twenties. I identified myself as a woman defined by those damaging experiences. That exchange rate was the only one I knew: "I was hurt, therefore I am hurt." And I meant it in two ways: that I was still hurting, and that hurt made me who I am.

Let's be clear. Sometimes people want to act as if nothing has happened to them, or they blow off the significance of what happened. I'm not talking about going to that extreme either. There is a big difference between acknowledging the hurt that has occurred and what you're doing to process and heal from it, and ignoring or minimizing your experience and acting like that's a form of healing. Think of it this way. If I keep picking at a scab, it's going to take a very long time to heal. If I treat the wound by washing it out, keeping it clean, and putting antibiotic cream on it, I'm acknowledging the wound and creating a good environment for healing.

But let's say I get a splinter under my skin, and I don't tell anyone about it because I don't want anyone to mess with it. Or I act like the discomfort of that splinter is no big deal, and I leave it in place. Over time, infection can set in. Scarring around that splinter can occur. There may be a period of time in which everything seems fine, but it isn't.

Picking at a wound or ignoring a wound has to be exchanged with seeking true healing. If we want to progress in our journey to that place where we allow God to deal with the injustices in our lives, this is the exchange rate we have to be willing to accept to enter that state.

Yes, you're hurt. Yes, choosing to move from that point of hurt into a process of healing can seem overwhelming. It can seem as if you're undermining the significance of what happened to you. You're not. You're entering new territory in which the God of restoration can begin to heal your life. This is one of the exchanges you will want to make to fully see how God is defending you: to exchange your identity as someone living in a state of hurt for someone moving to a state of healed.

## Exchange "I Don't Think It's Fair" for "I Can Release What's Fair and Accept What Is"

I've got to say, this is an exchange rate that I really struggled with, just like I told you back in chapter 3. I've lived some long days in the land of "I don't think it's fair," and it didn't get me any closer to where I wanted to be.

Exchange always involves letting go of something that is known and taking hold of something unknown. Think about when you exchange money: you trade the familiar dollar bills and coins you're used to, and you take hold of money that looks different and is counted in a different way. There's a release that happens when one kind of money leaves your hand and you receive a different kind of cash.

The exchange of "I don't think it's fair" for "I can release what's fair and accept what is" feels tricky. It can feel as if what we say we base our values on and our definitions of righteousness no longer matter. But please hear me: that's not it. I still have a very clear sense of what I think is fair and unfair. Look, the exchange of currency doesn't make the original currency invalid. It's simply adjusting the means by which you will navigate a different place. Your sense of fair is real, and it matters. But when you accept what is, even when it is unfair, you are able to move forward into what is real with a new power.

Continuing to reflect on the unfairness of a situation keeps you stuck there. But you and I are on the move toward knowing God even better and relying on and trusting in him even more. To do that, we need to make this exchange at the border of What

Has Been and What Can Be, walking fully into what is, fair and unfair alike.

As God's Word says at the end of Jesus' Sermon on the Mount, "[God] gives his sunlight to both the evil and the good, and he sends rain on the just and the unjust alike" (Matt. 5:45 NLT). But let's back up a verse or two to make sure we get the full context of what Jesus said here. Matthew 5:43–45 says, "You have heard the law that says, 'Love your neighbor' and hate your enemy. But I say, love your enemies! Pray for those who persecute you! In that way, you will be acting as true children of your Father in heaven" (NLT).

Is it fair that evil people receive the warmth of the sun? Maybe not. But God makes it shine on both the evil and the good. Is it fair that rain falls on the just? Perhaps not. But when we act like true children of God, we exchange evaluating it that way, we accept what is, and we make it our aim to reflect our Father.

### Exchange "I Can Never Let This Go" for "I Acknowledge What Happened, and I Can Move On"

Did you ever see *Groundhog Day*, the movie from the early nineties starring Bill Murray and Andie MacDowell? Bill Murray played the role of a TV weatherman sent to Punxsutawney, Pennsylvania, to cover February 2, Groundhog Day. Groundhog Day is a tradition that started in the United States. People gather to see if a groundhog can see his shadow on February 2. If the groundhog popping out of the ground does cast a shadow, then people say that winter will last six more weeks. But if the day is cloudy and there is no shadow when the groundhog comes out of its den, then the myth is that spring will come much sooner.

In the movie, Bill Murray's weatherman character has a really bad attitude about being sent to cover Groundhog Day.

He thinks the tradition is ridiculous, and he despises the town of Punxsutawney and its residents. He complains the whole day to his producer, played by Andie MacDowell, who is there to help him do the story. To make matters worse, a freak blizzard hits the town, and Bill Murray's character and his producer and cameraman are all trapped in Punxsutawney for the night.

The next morning, a strange thing happens. When Bill Murray's character is awakened by the clock radio, his day starts exactly as it did the day before. He has inexplicably become trapped in some weird loop, and he seems to be the only person who is aware of it. He lives Groundhog Day all over again, becoming increasingly frustrated and irritated with everything.

And it happens over and over and over again.

After some time of despair and suicidal tendencies, he tries something different. He begins to look for joy. He opens up to love. And ultimately, he exits that groundhog loop.[1]

It's a weird and wacky journey, and the message is clear: until he leaves selfishness behind, he is destined to repeat the same day over and over.

That's how it's felt when I have been willing to let go of some of the things that have come against me. Every day, I've started out with the same thoughts, the same anger, the same replay of what happened. But if we ever want to move into a brighter day, we have to honor the exchange rate. To move on, we have to let go of what was.

I look at the exchange rate listed in the book of Jeremiah. Jeremiah was a prophet in the Old Testament, and he spent much of his time encouraging the Israelites to exchange the discouragement and choices and bondage they were experiencing for something far better. He encouraged them with the better life God had in mind for them: "The young women will dance for joy, and the men—old and young—will join in the celebration. I will turn their mourning into joy. I will comfort them and exchange their sorrow for rejoicing" (Jer. 31:13 NLT). And the prophet Isaiah said that God would "bestow on them a crown of beauty instead of ashes, the oil of joy instead of mourning, and a garment of praise instead of a spirit of despair" (Isa. 61:3).

For the Israelites to leave a place of sadness, despair, and mourning, they had to first make sure God was their center, and then they had to be willing to let go of what had been to grasp what was ahead. I have spent far too long in certain seasons of my life repeating to myself what I wouldn't let go of instead of reaching toward what God had for me.

Can I encourage you? The past is over. Don't get stuck in a never-ending Groundhog Day. I'm not saying to forget what happened to you or that it didn't matter; it does. But exchange what was for the hope that God also has a future for you.

## Exchange "I Can Never Be the Same" for "I Have Grown and Matured from This"

Some of the hurts I experienced absolutely, irretrievably changed me. I wasn't the same after those experiences. When I was sexually abused as an eight-year-old, my virginity was taken from me. That's not something you can walk back.

It makes me think about Daniel, Shadrach, Meshach, and Abednego. They were four Hebrew boys taken from Israel into captivity in Babylon. When they arrived in Babylon, they underwent extensive training and modification to become servants in the royal household network. Now, the Bible doesn't tell us for sure, but historians say that many males who were enslaved by the Babylonians were castrated. This was especially true if they were made slaves in the household of the king, because it was of critical importance that children born in the palace were clearly descendants of the king.

Daniel 1:3–4 says,

> Then the king commanded Ashpenaz, his chief eunuch, to bring some of the people of Israel, both of the royal family and of the nobility, youths without blemish, of good appearance and skill-ful in all wisdom, endowed with knowledge, understanding learning, and competent to stand in the king's palace, and to teach them the literature and language of the Chaldeans. (ESV)

That means the king's chief eunuch was mentoring Daniel, Shadrach, Meshach, and Abednego, preparing them to serve in the same kind of position in the king's household. Additionally, a prophecy in 2 Kings 20:18 had said, "And some of your descendants, your own flesh and blood who will be born to you, will be taken away, and they will become eunuchs in the palace of the king of Babylon." Now that moment in history had arrived.

We can't know for sure if Daniel and his friends were cas-trated, but it does seem likely. If these four young guys—taken from their high-end neighborhoods and families of position, hauled to Babylon, and made slaves in the king's household—were castrated, that added the ultimate injury on top of everything else they had experienced. And just as when my virginity was violently taken from me as a child, these young men were forever altered as a result of what happened to them.

Yet all four of them continued to grow and flourish in their obedience and relationship to God. We read in Daniel 1:20 that "in every matter of wisdom and understanding about which the king inquired of them, he found them ten times better than all the magicians and enchanters that were in all his kingdom" (ESV).

You may have experienced something that forever altered you, physically or emotionally. You will bear the scars. But just as physical scars make the affected area tougher, so you can come through this experience stronger. Better, just like Daniel and his friends. It doesn't mean that you make light of what happened. Being sexually abused as a child changed me a lot. I'm not saying that we should say something ridiculous like "But I'm glad it happened because blah blah blah . . ." No. It's degrading to reduce what happened to me and what may have happened to you to that kind of ludicrous casualness. What I'm saying is that what God can do in your life, how he can make you stronger and wiser and more compassionate and more powerful in the wake of it, is miraculous. I know this because I've lived it. It began with exchanging what had changed me for letting God grow me and mature me. And he will do it for you too.

## Exchange "I Will Never Forgive" for "I, Through Christ, Can Do All Things"

This seems to be one of the costliest exchanges we will ever make. That's why I've left it for last in the "I for an I" list. We know as followers of Jesus that forgiveness is important. We know that we have been forgiven much and in turn should forgive much. We even know the math, that Jesus expects us to forgive at a rate of seventy times seven (Matt. 18:22 RSV).

But that doesn't make it any easier, at least for me.

Here's something that's a little weird: I sometimes find it harder to forgive the little things that happen to me. It's a holdover from the years I tried to ignore and bury the big things that happened to me, and as a young child and early tween, I thought keeping my mouth shut was a form of forgiveness. In later years, when someone would be a little harsh with me or would be difficult about something, I could find myself holding a grudge longer, because underneath, I had so much turmoil and so many unresolved emotions about the bigger stuff.

Forgiveness feels like letting someone off the hook. It feels that way because—wait for it—it *is* letting someone off the hook. Yep. You are releasing someone from the emotional position you've been holding them in. Now let's be clear about what forgiveness is and isn't. Forgiveness isn't about releasing someone from accountability. You can forgive and still report someone's illegal behavior to authorities. You can forgive and still choose not to put yourself in someone's path again. That was my mistake for years: what I thought it meant for me to walk in forgiveness. I believed that letting someone off the hook in my heart also meant letting that person off the hook for the legal and relational consequences that might follow.

Thinking of forgiveness as an exchange helps me. It's not an exchange in which the other person might finally apologize. It's not an exchange in which the other party might make things right. And it's not an exchange in which the other party might avoid the legal or relational ramifications that are sometimes the result of wrong behavior.

It is an exchange in which I learn just how powerful Christ in me is. It is an exchange in which I can stand in wonder at how God can heal me and release me from the hold of someone who has wronged me. And it is an exchange that pays incredible interest in return. I want big forgiveness in my life from God, and Jesus said that my willingness to forgive is directly connected to God's forgiveness of me.

There's something else I've learned about forgiveness: it's not a one-time event. I've forgiven people in my life who deeply wronged me—and I forgive them again in this moment. I'm betting I'll forgive them again tomorrow, all for the same things they did to me years ago. I have to actively maintain that forgiveness. For a long time, I thought that if I was forgiving "correctly," I could forgive once and be done. But I think that's part of what Jesus was saying when he gave the math of forgiveness:

> Peter came up and said to him, "Lord, how often shall my brother sin against me, and I forgive him? As many as seven times?" Jesus said to him, "I do not say to you seven times, but seventy times seven." (Matt. 18:21–22 RSV)

I used to read this thinking it meant that if someone sins against you on seventy-times-seven occasions, then you are to forgive that person for each occasion. And maybe that is what it means. But to me it also means that when a hurt comes bubbling up, when the person who hurt me is at the extended-family event or at a social gathering, I need to continue that forgiveness. I may have to keep forgiving someone for hurting me, and it may take me a number of times to develop a habit of forgiving that person.

Here's another value of the exchange rate: I stand in awe of what Jesus has done when I extend forgiveness to others. There are things that make me know to my core that there is a God. A newborn baby. The ocean crashing against the beach. And the fact that Christ has empowered me to forgive people who absolutely didn't deserve it and didn't even value it. It's miraculous the way he can help us do this. This exchange rate is critical in our journey of seeing God as our Defender because forgiveness is the currency of heaven.

These five exchanges most likely won't come easy for you. It makes sense to us to repay hurt with hurt when someone harms us. It satisfies our sense of retribution to repay rejection with rejection. We think we'll find relief by repaying someone who has caused us loss by creating a loss on that person's side. Peter knew that we would find it tempting to try to avoid the process of receiving new currency through an exchange process. He knew we would be tempted to keep paying out, dollar for dollar, what was doled out to us. But his warning still stands through the ages, as does the promise: "Do not repay evil with evil or insult with insult. On the contrary, repay evil with blessing, because to this you were called so that you may inherit a blessing" (1 Peter 3:9).

I know how you're used to paying for the wrongs you've experienced. I know it could feel safer to stay with what is familiar. But those exchange rates only keep us lingering longer at the border, caught in a land that has held only pain for us, when healing and purpose lie just on the other side.

Trade your burdens. Trade your broken heart. Trade your loss. And receive fresh eyes, a renewed faith, an empowered story. He is able. He is *so* able. That is true restoration that surpasses any amount of revenge, vindication, or repayment.

*conclusion*

# HOW YOU KNOW

AT LAST, WE ARRIVE HERE.

You've navigated some pretty treacherous waters, friend. You've had to look directly into the original situation that wounded you so badly. You've had to accept the assignment that to experience God as your Defender, you need to address the battle within yourself. You've had to sort through your own sense of fair and unfair. You've had to identify the Isle of Idolatry where perhaps you ran aground. You've learned to stop struggling in the Quicksand of Self-Destruction and allow grace to lift you out. You've reevaluated those windmill dragons you've been battling. You've traveled through the dark shadows of the Ravine of Vindication and learned how to exit the Trap of Avoidance. You've embraced the best kind of revenge, the kind in which you reclaim afresh the abundant life Jesus has for you. You've learned about the attributes of Jehovah El Elyon, God my Shield, God my Defender, and you've seen that his defensive methods can look different from your expectations. You've learned the exchange rate of true restoration.

You have persevered.

And here we are.

Which leaves us with a question, doesn't it?

How do we know? How do we truly know that we have fully embraced God as our Defender?

There's one test that remains, and it may not be one you're willing to take. That may be okay for now. Believe me when I tell you that it will leave you stuck back at one of the places we've passed through in this book. It is the one thing standing between you and the full understanding of God as your Defender. But it's okay if it takes you a while to face it. This last test is a tough one. It will be here when you're ready.

But can I just ask you, please, to try? Ask the Holy Spirit to guide you through this. Keep reading and see what the Holy Spirit guides you to do.

## WITH ALL MY HEART

Corrie ten Boom's journey was so intense, it's hard to comprehend. She was a Dutch Christian living in the Netherlands, and she had a career as a watchmaker. As a matter of fact, at the age of thirty-two, she was the first woman licensed as a watchmaker in the Netherlands.

She was in her late forties when Adolf Hitler came into power in Germany. The Netherlands at that time was considered a neutral country in all the turmoil swirling around it, much the way Switzerland remains neutral in many world affairs. But Hitler chose to invade the Netherlands anyway in the spring of 1940.

Corrie was living with her sister Betsie and their widowed father. Initially, after the German invasion, life continued in a somewhat normal fashion. But over time, the economic situation became more desperate. Then began more severe persecution of the Jewish people of the Netherlands.

One day a woman came to the Ten Booms' watch-repair shop asking for help. Her husband had already been arrested for being Jewish, and their son had gone into hiding. The woman knew she was at significant risk of being taken. The Ten Booms agreed to take her in, and over time, they took in others as well. A secret room was built in Corrie's upstairs bedroom, and several Jewish people took shelter there.

Eventually, after two years, the authorities found out about the Ten Booms' underground network.

Corrie, Betsie, and their father were all arrested and sent to prison. Corrie's father, Casper, died only ten days after his arrest, and months later, Betsie and Corrie were moved first to a concentration camp and then to the death camp Ravensbrück, where Betsie died. Following Betsie's death, Corrie was released from Ravensbrück, almost a year after their arrest. She went on to write and speak about her experiences and the atrocities she had suffered at the hands of her Nazi guards, along with the hope with which God had sustained her.

Years later, while at a speaking engagement, she came face-to-face with one of the guards who had been most heinous to her. In that moment, she was faced with the realization that while she had navigated many hurdles after her release, hurdles like the ones you and I have overcome in this book, one hurdle remained.

The former guard approached her, wanting to shake her hand and thank her for the powerful talk she had given on the forgiveness of God. She knew immediately who he was, and all the memories came flooding back. She remembered the leather crop he had carried and used. She remembered the uniform he had worn, with its Nazi insignia, and the cap he had worn with a skull-and-crossbones patch, the *Totenkopf* symbol displayed on the hats of the guards. In a flash, she remembered it all.

He didn't recognize her.

She wrote this about what was going through her mind and heart:

And still I stood there with the coldness clutching my heart. But forgiveness is not an emotion—I knew that too. Forgiveness is an act of the will, and the will can function regardless of the temperature of the heart.

"Jesus, help me!" I prayed silently. "I can lift my hand. I can do that much. You supply the feeling."

And so woodenly, mechanically, I thrust my hand into the one stretched out to me. And as I did, an incredible thing took place. The current started in my shoulder, raced down my arm, sprang into our joined hands. And then this healing warmth seemed to flood my whole being, bringing tears to my eyes.

"I forgive you, brother!" I cried. "With all my heart!"

For a long moment we grasped each other's hands, the former guard and the former prisoner. I had never known God's love so intensely as I did then.[1]

Yeah. This is next level.

But it is the place where we show we have fully accepted God as our Defender. When we can release the one who has harmed us into the arms of a forgiving God.

We often withhold forgiveness as a form of revenge. Oh, you may not actively retaliate against someone. You may hold your tongue when you have a chance to gossip. You may stay out of the fray. You may keep your mouth shut and stand back. But are you waiting to forgive until you see God deal with the person who hurt you?

It's the last hurdle in the journey toward trusting God as your Defender. And it's the place where many of us get ensnared for a good long time. It's particularly true when it comes to those hurts that seem the most horrendous—wrongs like sexual abuse, assault, bodily injury, or financial ruin. We want people to earn forgiveness. We want them to pay a price for it, because, let's face it, forgiveness can cost us dearly. But it also costs us dearly to withhold it.

Right now, you may not yet be at a place where you can accept this final step of trusting God as your Defender. The cost may seem too high to you. But it's the exchange we talked about in chapter 11 that is central to true restoration.

Please don't miss what Corrie said happened when she made this exchange. She said she had never known God's love as intensely as she did then. His perfect love that can seem invisible to us became fully known to her in that moment. In that moment, her eyes were opened to the army of heaven that surrounded her through all the pain and all the questions, and God's love was made known.

To know God as your Defender means praying that he will let you heal and forgive with all your heart. The heart entrusted into his hands is his mighty weapon, and your heart will be safe there when God is your Defender.

## OPEN MY EYES

The king of Aram was a busy guy who was at war with the nation of Israel. And he had a big problem: wherever he tried to camp out with his troops, it seemed that the king of Israel was always able to find them. No matter how great a hiding spot he found, in short order, his army would be found out. He was furious and frustrated.

He demanded that his men figure out how this kept happening. One of them let him know that the king of Israel had a secret weapon: the prophet Elisha. It was Elisha who kept the king of Israel informed as to all the movements of the Aramean army.

The king of Aram was enraged. He ordered a number of his troops to bring this pesky Elisha guy to him.

The troops found Elisha at Dothan and circled the city during the night, ready to swoop in the next day and grab him. Elisha's assistant went out that morning and realized the city was surrounded. He came running back to Elisha to warn him. "'Oh no, my lord! What shall we do?' the servant asked" (2 Kings 6:15).

Elisha didn't go slam and lock the shutters. He didn't try to bargain. He didn't run for the hills. Instead, the prophet told his servant,

> "Don't be afraid. . . . Those who are with us are more than those who are with them." And Elisha prayed, "Open his eyes, LORD, so that he may see." Then the LORD opened the servant's eyes, and he looked and saw the hills full of horses and chariots of fire all around Elisha. (vv. 16–17)

I can get so focused on the enemy coming for me that I can miss the army that surrounds me. To understand God as your Defender, ask him to open your eyes to see. Too often I've looked only for what is coming against me instead of looking for what is for me. To see God as your Defender, you'll have to look with different eyes. You'll have to pray a different prayer. Open your eyes through the power of God.

## THIS IS HOW I FIGHT MY BATTLES

Elyssa Smith is part of a ministry called UPPERROOM. One day, as members of that ministry were meeting together, Elyssa was inspired to write a song.[2]

The story they were reading from 2 Chronicles was about a time when the king of the Israelites, Jehoshaphat, sent his army out to face their enemy. But instead of putting his biggest weapons or best swordsmen or strongest shields at the front of the army, he sent the Levites out front and told them to sing songs of worship as they headed into battle. It makes me think about some concepts we discussed earlier, like the power of worshiping together and practicing the best kind of revenge. Jehoshaphat knew the power of worship and said that it would confuse the enemy army.

And it did. The opposing armies began slaughtering each other. By the time the army of Israel arrived, it was all over.

Would you like to know what the Levites were singing?

Yeah, I thought you might.

They sang, "Give thanks to the Lord, for his love endures forever" (2 Chron. 20:21).

The Word says that as they sang, God created an ambush that set the enemy armies against each other. That is an incredible display of God as our Defender. God's people didn't have to raise a physical weapon. They didn't have to use military might or tactics.

But they did use the one thing the enemy didn't: praise. And not just any praise—a praise of thanksgiving to God and a reminder that his love is limitless and eternal.

Now back to the songwriter Elyssa Smith. As she and her team talked about this passage from 2 Chronicles, they also began to discuss the passage about Elisha from 2 Kings 6 that we looked at a little earlier. And Elyssa began to write a very special song.

The lyrics are pretty simple, but if you've heard it, then you know how powerful it is. It's called "Surrounded (Fight My Battles)." The chorus says,

It may look like I'm surrounded

But I'm surrounded by you.

This is how I fight my battles.

Dealing with our emotions and the consequences we experience when we have been wronged is complicated. Inviting God in as our Defender is not. You are surrounded by a lot. The person who hurt you. The situation that led up to it. The fallout from that experience. The feelings you carry. Those are all real. They matter.

But you are also surrounded by a God who loves you, a God who doesn't expect you to go into battle alone.

All through his Word, God has given us reminders that he is with us, he battles for us, and he is for us. He reassured the Israelites as he guided them toward the promised land, "For the LORD your God is the one who goes with you to fight for you against your enemies to give you victory" (Deut. 20:4). He reminded the early Christians who were facing persecution, "What, then, shall we say in response to these things? If God is for us, who can be against us?" (Rom. 8:31).

And he is with us even today.

This is how you fight your battles: with God going before you and doing it his way, with timing that may befuddle you, with a purpose you may not always understand, and with a mix of justice and mercy that are completely his own. You will find healing. You will find rest. You will be given vindication and restoration. And you will find peace.

I leave you with the words of King David, the writer of the imprecatory psalms we talked about all the way back in chapter 1. The same David wrote Psalm 23, which is arguably his most famous writing. It's a psalm that people the world over can quote, even those who don't yet know God as Father like you and I do. Some scholars argue that David wrote Psalm 23 later in his life, at a time when enemies were threatening him, in perhaps one of his darkest moments. It shows a man who, through walking closely with God for so long, had learned about what God the Defender can do and the promise that his love brings.

> You prepare a feast for me
>> in the presence of my enemies.
> You honor me by anointing my head with oil.
>> My cup overflows with blessings.
> Surely your goodness and unfailing love will pursue me
>> all the days of my life,
> and I will live in the house of the LORD
>> forever. (Ps. 23:5–6 NLT)

God's goodness chases you. His unfailing love pursues you. He serves you and honors you in front of those who act as your enemies. And he has secured eternity for you.

When you live knowing this, then you know that you have come through the places that would seek to distract you from this truth. You have learned the lessons of all the stops along the way. After all, the ultimate destination of this journey, from the moment you were hurt until now, has been to bring you home to your God.

God is your Defender. Let him do what he does best.

# ACKNOWLEDGMENTS

LITTLE-GIRL DREAMS COME TRUE BECAUSE OF WON-
derful people like you, Beth Davey. Thank you for not only being
my agent but also for being my cheerleader every step of the way.

This book would not have been possible without you, Julie Carr.
You captured my voice and message in the most beautiful way. Thank
you for your patience and sharing your talent with me.

Betty Meza, my amazing manager, thank you for advocating for
this book before anyone else did and for dreaming little-girl dreams
with me. See you on the Staples Center stage, and many other plat-
forms. You are a friend, a voice of influence, and the exhortation I
need in my life.

Thank you so much to Beth, Stephanie, Meaghan, Darcie, and
everyone else at W Publishing and HarperCollins. I could not have
imagined a more caring, detail-oriented, and supportive team. I am
blessed to have you on this journey. Thank you, HarperCollins, for
receiving me. I wasn't going to quit until you did. I'm grateful that it
is now.

# NOTES

## Chapter 2: Going on the Journey

1. Zoe Mitchell, "Candy Land," American Experience on PBS, July 13, 2018, https://www.pbs.org/wgbh/americanexperience /features/candy-land/.

## Chapter 3: The Spiral of Fair

1. "Joan of Arc," History.com, November 9, 2009, https://www .history.com/topics/middle-ages/saint-joan-of-arc.

## Chapter 4: The Isles of Idolatry

1. Blue Letter Bible, s.v. "pathos," from *Strong's Concordance*, accessed June 16, 2020, https://www.blueletterbible.org/lang /lexicon/lexicon.cfm?Strongs=G3806&t=kjv.
2. Clinton E. Arnold, *The Colossian Syncretism: The Interface Between Christianity and Folk Belief at Colossae* (Tübingen, Germany: J.C.B. Mohr, 1995), 21–23, https://www .mohrsiebeck.com/uploads/tx_sgpublisher/produkte /leseproben/9783161571237.pdf.
3. Candice Lucey, "Who Is the Archangel Michael?" Christianity .com, January 23, 2020, https://www.christianity.com/wiki /angels-and-demons/who-is-the-archangel-michael.html.
4. Wikipedia, s.v. "Adrestia," last modified July 18, 2020, https:// en.wikipedia.org/wiki/Adrestia.
5. Wikipedia, s.v. "Iturbide, Nuevo León," last updated March 1, 2020, https://en.wikipedia.org/wiki/Iturbide,_Nuevo _Le%C3%B3n.

## Chapter 5: The Quicksand of Self-Destruction

1. Jeremy Taylor, *The Sermons of the Right Rev. Jeremy Taylor, D.D., Lord Bishop of Down, Connor, and Dromore* (New York: Robert Carter & Brothers, 1852), 143.

2. Lena Welch, "Will Quicksand Kill You? The Science of Goo: Cornstarch, Quicksand, Oobleck, and Non-Newtonian Fluids," Owlcation, April 24, 2020, https://owlcation.com/stem /Oobleck-Quicksand-Cornstarch-And-Water.

## Chapter 6: The Pitfall of Windmills

1. Marianne Bonner, "Most Ridiculous Lawsuits," The Balance Small Business, December 10, 2019, https://www.thebalancesmb .com/most-ridiculous-lawsuits-of-all-time-4110919.

## Chapter 7: The Ravine of Vindication

1. David B. Feldman, "Why Do People Blame the Victim?" *Psychology Today*, March 2, 2018, https://www .psychologytoday.com/us/blog/supersurvivors/201803 /why-do-people-blame-the-victim.
2. "Ex-husband of Latina Singer Gets 31 Years for Molestation," *Press-Telegram*, June 20, 2007, https://www.presstelegram .com/2007/06/20/ex-husband-of-latina-singer-gets-31-years -for-molestation/.

## Chapter 8: The Trap of Avoidance

1. Marla Carter, "Twelve Alleged Abuse Cases at Texas Summer Camps Uncovered," *ABC 13 Eyewitness News*, May 1, 2019, https://abc13.com/12-alleged-abuse-cases-at-texas-summer -camps-uncovered/5281234/.

## Chapter 9: Practice the Best Revenge

1. "Living Well Is the Best Revenge," Quote Investigator, accessed June 22, 2020, https://quoteinvestigator.com/2018/09/02 /living-well/.
2. Christine Ammer, *The Dictionary of Clichés* (New York: Skyhorse Publishing, 2013), 127.

## Chapter 10: The Ultimate Defender

1. Christina Proctor, "Tougher Penalties for State's Sex Offenders," *Tahoe Daily Tribune*, December 19, 2001, https://www

.tahoedailytribune.com/news/tougher-penalties
-for-states-sex-offenders/.

2. Online Etymology Dictionary, s.v. "gloat," accessed June 25, 2020, https://www.etymonline.com/search?q=gloat.

## Chapter 11: True Restoration

1. *Groundhog Day*, directed by Harold Ramis, written by Danny Rubin, featuring Bill Murray and Andie MacDowell (Culver City, CA: Columbia Pictures, 1993).

## Conclusion: How You Know

1. Corrie ten Boom, "Guidepost Classics: Corrie ten Boom on Forgiveness," *Guideposts*, July 24, 2014, https://www.guideposts.org/better-living/positive-living/guideposts-classics-corrie-ten-boom-on-forgiveness.

2. Kevin Davis, "#926: 'Surrounded (Fight My Battles)' by UPPERROOM," New Release Today, June 20, 2018, https://www.newreleasetoday.com/article.php?article_id=2422.

# ABOUT THE AUTHOR

**ROSIE RIVERA** IS AN AUTHOR, AN ENTREPRENEUR, AND the testamentary executor of Jenni Rivera Enterprises, as well as an international speaker and influential public figure. Rosie uses her platform to lift up, motivate, and give hope to sexual abuse victims as a survivor and counselor.

Rosie has cohosted top Spanish morning shows such as *Despierta América* and *Un Nuevo Día* and cohosts, along with her husband, a marriage podcast called *The Power of Us* on reVolver Podcast. Rosie has participated and starred in reality shows such as *I Love Jenni*, *The Riveras*, *Mira Quién Baila*, and *Rica Famosa Latina*, currently on Netflix.

Rosie is happily married to singer-songwriter and worshiper Abel Flores. The couple lives in Lakewood, California, where they raise their three children, Kassey, Sammy, and Eli.